KT-368-165

Business Planning

A guide to business start-up

David Butler

NORWICH CITY COLLEGE LIBRARY		
Stock No.	224035	
Class	658.022 BUT	
Cat.	AMx2 m	Proc. 3wh

ELSEVIER
BUTTERWORTH
HEINEMANN

AMSTERDAM • BOSTON • HEIDELBERG • LONDON • NEW YORK • OXFORD
PARIS • SAN DIEGO • SAN FRANCISCO • SINGAPORE • SYDNEY • TOKYO

Elsevier Butterworth Heinemann
Linacre House, Jordan Hill, Oxford OX2 8DP
200 Wheeler Road, Burlington, MA 01803

First published 2000
Transferred to digital printing 2003

Copyright © 2000, David Butler. All rights reserved

The right of David Butler to be identified as the author of this work has been
asserted in accordance with the Copyright, Designs and Patents Act 1988

No part of this publication may be reproduced in any material form (including
photocopying or storing in any medium by electronic means and whether
or not transiently or incidentally to some other use of this publication) without
the written permission of the copyright holder except in accordance with the
provisions of the Copyright, Designs and Patents Act 1988 or under the terms of
a licence issued by the Copyright Licensing Agency Ltd, 90 Tottenham Court Road,
London, England WIT 4LP. Applications for the copyright holder's written
permission to reproduce any part of this publication should be addressed
to the publisher

Permissions may be sought directly from Elsevier's Science & Technology Rights
Department in Oxford, UK: phone: (+44) 1865 843830, fax: (+44) 1865 853333,
e-mail: permissions@elsevier.co.uk. You may also complete your request on-line via
the Elsevier homepage (http://www.elsevier.com), by selecting 'Customer Support'
and then 'Obtaining Permissions'

British Library Cataloguing in Publication Data
Butler, David
    Business Planning: a guide to business start-up
    1. New Business Enterprises – Planning   2. Business Planning
    I. Title
    658.1'141

Library of Congress Cataloguing in Publication Data
A catalogue record for this book is available from the Library of Congress

ISBN 0 7506 4706 X

For information on all Elsevier Butterworth-Heinemann
publications visit our website at www.bh.com

CONTENTS

Contents

Preface
Preface

Preface

Much of the contents of this book are based on empirical experience – been there, done it, got the T-shirt, and learnt by my own mistakes over a fifteen-year period; and so I hope that by passing on this experience, I might save the readers some grief of their own. The book is intended to serve two key purposes, which for many of its target audience, will overlap each other.

First, it is intended as a course textbook for students and candidates who are studying for either the NVQ Level 3 Business Planning, or the Institute of Management Certificate in Management (Business Start-up), which closely follows the content and syllabus of the NVQ. The Vocational Standards for the NVQ Level 3 Business Planning were revised in 1999 by the Small Firms Enterprise Development Initiative (SFEDI). The SFEDI, alongside the Management Charter Initiative (MCI), is a partner in the Management and Enterprise Training Organization (METO) which has incorporated the lead-body roles of these two organizations under one umbrella, and is now responsible for establishing the national vocational standards for all aspects of management.

The book is intended both to provide the basic factual information necessary to gain the underpinning knowledge to achieve the NVQ, along with advice and guidance on the preparation of suitable portfolio evidence which will enable the candidate to be successfully assessed for the NVQ or Certificate qualifications. In producing the necessary evidence requirements to meet the NVQ assessment process, the candidates will also produce for themselves, a feasible business plan which is capable of being lifted directly out of the NVQ portfolio for presentation to a bank manager, or an alternative potential source of finance.

Second, and on a much more practical level, the book is aimed at providing a readable and structured guide for the increasing numbers of people who each year consider the option of setting up a small business or becoming self-employed. It outlines the options for operating the business and the many risks involved. It also examines a wide range of aspects that must be considered and assessed as part of the process of setting up a business. For those aspiring owner-managers, the information about NVQ structure and assessment is unlikely to be of much interest. But whether the reader's objective is to produce a business plan to simply achieve a qualification, or to produce such a document to convince a dubious bank manager of the viability of a business proposition, many of the key aspects to be considered are the same. Most important of all, a careful and detailed analysis of those aspects can provide a yardstick by which potential entrepreneurs can objectively evaluate the true risks, pitfalls and potential profits of their dreams.

The book has been deliberately formulated to raise a continuous stream of questions throughout, which are intended to prompt the reader to relate them to their own particular business situation. If you keep asking yourself these questions at each stage, then hopefully you will avoid some of the problems that befall many new businesses in the early stages.

The biggest problem faced by small firms is that of surviving the first year or two. A basic knowledge of the process of planning and organizing a business can substantially increase the chances of survival, with or without the accompanying qualifications. This book is aimed at providing some of that knowledge and information to improve those chances. Good luck with your venture!

David Butler

Chapter 1 The importance of business planning

Chapter 1
Chapter 1

Why should I bother with a business plan?

There is a whole host of reasons to justify the preparation of business plans, not just for business start-up enterprises, but as a model of good practice for established organizations. Any one of these reasons in its own right should make the planning process a worthwhile exercise, if it is done properly. However, the important thing to remember, is that just producing a good business plan alone, will not result in a sound, profitable or prosperous business. The business plan is just that – a plan – and like any other plan, the only way to see if it really works is to monitor its progress at regular intervals, so that you can respond to any potential problems which may arise and then change or modify your business strategy as necessary. So, let us have a look at some of the reasons why people take the trouble to produce business plans.

First, the process of producing a business plan acts as a very efficient method of focusing the ideas of potential entrepreneurs in terms of defining their objectives and assessing their own abilities to organize and run the business. It also acts as a means of testing the viability of the business proposal before actually committing its proposers to any substantial expenditure or investment. Typically, this type of plan would be prepared before the start-up or acquisition of the business.

Second, the planning process establishes parameters and specific targets which provide a yardstick against which the progress and profitability of the business can be measured. Again, this planning activity is a prerequisite to starting or acquiring a business but, beyond that, it is also part of the ongoing process of running a business which should be continued as an ongoing process, long after the initial start-up.

Third, as there are relatively few aspiring entrepreneurs who have the resources to be totally self-financing, most are faced at some time with the need to raise external finance, if not at the start-up stage then later when they wish to expand and grow the established business. For these persons, possession of a good business plan is crucial to their future; their appointment with the financier or bank manager to discuss the proposal is a bit like an audition for a part in a Hollywood film – if you blow your lines you blow your chances or, at least, you reduce your prospects of getting the part you really want! So it is most important to prepare the plan thoroughly, and to present it in a professional and competent manner.

The business plan as a means of focusing ideas

The production of a comprehensive business plan is really centred on a process of questions and answers; and the deeper you move into the plan, the more questions arise which must be answered. Most people who are considering buying or setting up a business, or becoming self-employed, have a fairly general idea of what they would like to achieve. Typically this may take the form of a range of activities or options, perhaps linked in some way, or built around a central idea. It is only when someone asks them the question 'What are your specific objectives?' that they actually start to define the precise parameters within which their proposed business will operate. Typically, this question is only asked for the first time when they start to fill in the bank's business plan form. The primary objectives (often called the mission statement) of the business need to state clearly and specifically, the purpose for which the business exists, and the market in which it will operate. For example, 'I intend to operate a high-quality and profitable mobile catering service specializing in wedding receptions and private parties in the Kent and Sussex area' or, 'We will be providing a service which designs, constructs and maintains heated swimming pools for large private homes in London and the South East'. Invariably, statements such as these will invoke the immediate question 'How will this be achieved?' and leads the budding entrepreneur into the examination and explanation of the financial, operational, marketing and control aspects of the proposition, which forms the core of the business plan.

The next aspect which our new business person must consider is the viability of the proposition, and yet another question: 'Yes, it sound like a good idea, but what makes you think it will work?' Unfortunately, hunches, gut feelings, innate beliefs and even feminine intuition, cannot guarantee the viability of a business venture, so in answering the question we must offer some more tangible ideas, e.g. 'I am offering a service for which there is a growing awareness and demand and, at the current time, the nearest alternative supplier is located 100 miles away'. Viability may involve a range of considerations including market research and segmentation, feasibility studies, assessment of potential sales turnover and profit margins, breakeven analysis, availability of regular supplies, availability of competent staff, adequate working capital etc. Again, our budding entrepreneur is required to focus in much more detail on the practicalities of the proposition, not the least of which is his or her own personal skills. The subject of business viability will be examined in more detail in Chapter 3.

The business idea itself may be perfectly viable for any competent or experienced business person, but the other area which must be considered is whether or not our budding entrepreneur actually has the necessary skills and competencies to pull it off. Does the person have the necessary technical knowledge of the product or service? Do they have knowledge of the market? Have they had any sales experience? Can they manage people and delegate work? Do they have the necessary financial skills for book-keeping and credit control?

If any of these skills are lacking, can they be acquired in time, or will it be necessary to buy them in and, if so, can they afford the cost? The biggest single difference between managers of large firms and those of small firms, is that the large-company manager can afford to be a specialist, and can usually tap into someone else in the organization if there is a skills shortage in a specific area, e.g. finance or marketing. In contrast, in the small firm, the manager needs a breadth of general business skills, as well as a depth of knowledge of the product or service. Barclays Bank (1998) highlighted the fact that business owners only seem to appreciate the skills required to run a small business once they have experienced it for themselves. Less than one-third of business owners undertake any basic business skills training prior to starting up, with 80 per cent of the others believing that they already have adequate business skills to manage their business ventures.

However, personal aptitude is not just a question of possessing a broad range of basic business skills. The clearing banks have recognized this in the past few years and, as a result, have started to incorporate questions into their standard business plan forms which relate to personal skills, i.e. the management of yourself and your time. For example questions such as: are you self-motivated? Are you persistent, or do you give up easily? Can you take responsibility? Do you find it easy to make decisions? Are you a good organizer? Can you lead and motivate others? These again are aspects which can be developed and explained within your business plan as part of your personal profile and action plan. The business plan gives you the opportunity to emphasize your personal strengths in these areas, and to propose how you intend to improve on those skills that are not so strong. Those who ignore these questions, do so at their peril; as the lending banks are unlikely to have any sympathy with someone who cannot answer these questions openly and honestly, and admit to their own weaknesses.

It is interesting that in a survey carried out by Cranfield Management School on behalf of the Small Firms Enterprise Development Initiative (1998), contact was made with 1000 firms that had recently closed down. Of those, some 70 per cent claimed to have lacked the basic business skills they needed to survive. The business planning process provides an ideal opportunity to assess the range of skills which are needed in order for the business to succeed and, at the same time, identify any potential gaps within that range. The subject of self-assessment and self-appraisal is covered in more depth in Chapter 4.

The business plan as a yardstick to measure progress and achievement

As explained above, it is imperative that every new business has clearly defined objectives and parameters within which it will operate, however it is not sufficient for these to be expressed simply as bland statements. In order for us to be able to determine whether or not the objectives are being achieved, it is necessary to define them in much more detail. This is achieved through the process of financial planning (Chapter 6) and by the preparation of marketing plans (Chapter 9). These plans provide us with specific measurable targets against which we can compare and monitor progress and achievement on an ongoing basis, for example:

- Annual budgetary plans, forecasting income and expenditure on a month by month basis, against which actual income and expenditure can be monitored.

- Forecasts of gross profit margins and net profit margins derived from the budgetary plans, which can be monitored to pick up any problems due to rising costs, falling sales, or seasonal fluctuations in sales, etc.

5

- The effects of specific sales or promotional activities on sales revenues or profit margins.

- Cash flow forecasts, and the effects of giving or taking credit.

- The need for additional working capital to sustain business, e.g. by means of short-term overdrafts; or longer-term loans to facilitate expansion of the business.

- Affordability of capital investment – do we replace or repair? Do we produce components ourselves, or buy in? Do we use loans or hire purchase to buy equipment, or do we lease?

The planning and monitoring of progress and achievement is an integral part of the formulation of business policy. The initial business idea formulates the initial policies which determine the financial and marketing plans and targets. Achievement of those targets, or modifications to the plans in response to external influences and change, will influence the resources available for the future, which will in turn have a bearing on future business policy. This is the constant cycle of Plan, Implement, Monitor and Revise, although ideally, the revisions should take the form of proactive plans made in anticipation of future events, rather than a series of reactions in response to past events or circumstances.

Raising finance for start-up or expansion

As we have already considered, very few start-up businesses (apart, that is, from some self-employed trades, or ex-lottery winners!) have the luxury of not needing some form of finance, if not at the outset of trading, then later as the business starts to expand and grow. Even those not requiring funding are sometimes asked to provide a basic business plan in order to qualify for the initial period of free bank charges on their business bank accounts.

The various potential sources of business finance are discussed in Chapter 8, but for the great majority of small firms, the first port of call is their local bank manager. Inevitably, the first question asked of our budding entrepreneur is 'Can I see your Business Plan?' (a question which is usually closely followed by 'What forms of security or collateral can you offer?'). The simple fact of the matter is that these days banks will not readily lend to anyone who cannot present them with a viable business plan. Fortunately, this requirement also constitutes a much more responsible attitude to lending on the part of the banks; who at one time in the 1980s, were frequently accused of being willing to lend to anyone with adequate security, irrespective of the viability of their business proposition. When the going became tough, some bank managers simply closed down the struggling small businesses and called in their security against their loans.

Today, the clearing banks take a much more responsible attitude to potential business customers, and this is reflected in the questions which are asked within their standard business plan packs. The business plan has become an essential pre-requisite of any dialogue with the bank manager and forms the core means of assessing the prospects of survival and growth of any business. This attitude is best illustrated by three extracts from current customer information packs for business start-up issued by three of these banks:

A well-presented business plan will show if you have a viable idea, and a sound business-like approach to making something of it.
(Lloyds [TSB] Bank plc, 1998, p. 9)

A business plan sets out your objectives, estimates and financial forecasts. It will help you establish where you are, where you are going, and how you intend to get there. A well prepared business plan demonstrates your determination to start a successful business. It will help convince your

bank manager, suppliers, and contacts, that you know what you are doing.
(Midland Bank plc [HSBC], 1999, p. 11)

According to statistics taken from VAT [value added tax] records, only half of new businesses survive more than five years. The better your planning is, the more likely you are to succeed.
(NatWest Bank and Durham University Business School, 1995, p. 2)

The ability to prepare a comprehensive and coherent business plan is an absolute imperative for anyone starting in business, and particularly if finance is required from outside the business. Preparing a plan is not too difficult, given the many standard formats which are available these days; but preparing a *good* business plan requires a great deal of careful thought and effort. Take a look from the point of view of the bank manager; he or she is charged with the responsibility of controlling money which other people (possibly including yourself) have invested in the bank, and using that money to generate a profit. How would you feel if the bank manager went down to the local bookmakers and 'invested' your money on an outsider in the 2.30 p.m. horse race at Haydock Park – you would most definitely not be very impressed. From the bank manager's view, it is your business plan that reduces your chances of winning from those of a rank outsider to those of an odds-on favourite, or at least to an even chance. Your business proposal provides the bank manager with a risk analysis of your prospects, so it is in the interests of both of you to take all practical precautions to minimize those risks. You do so by preparing a detailed and comprehensive business plan, and the bank manager does his or her part by checking it objectively for potential hazards and risks, before lending you any money.

How often should I update my business plan?

Most business plans are updated on an annual basis. For most small firms it is unrealistic to prepare budgets and cash flow forecasts for more than a year ahead, but preparing them for less than a full year would be too short a time to generate useful information. Some firms revise their plans at the half-year stage if there look like being any major changes afoot.

The important thing to remember is that business planning is an ongoing process – it is not just something you prepare for the bank manager at the start of the year, and then throw in the filing cabinet and forget it until next time around. Plans need to be monitored on a regular and frequent basis if they are to be of any productive use. Budget outcomes (actual figures) should be compared with forecast figures at least once each month, and then within two weeks of the end of the month. This will enable prompt identification of any major discrepancies or problems which lie on the horizon. When discrepancies occur they must be questioned: why has this happened? Is it a one-off occurrence, or the start of a longer-term trend and potential problem? What has to be done to resolve the situation? Unfortunately, too many people faced with apparent problems are more concerned with asking 'Who is to blame?' rather than identifying the cause of the problems and working to find a solution. The subject of monitoring and control will be examined in more detail in Chapter 10.

One other aspect which must be considered here is the fundamentally different approach to planning by small firms compared with their big-company counterparts. Welch (1995, p. 3) states that 'the big-company model of managing and career development does not apply to small businesses'. Larger organizations have the resources, stability and security to facilitate the luxury of long-term strategic planning, perhaps three to five years ahead or possibly more, and the immediate year ahead is seen as the short term. For the owner-managers of small firms, the immediate problem is often simply one of survival – where is the next order coming from? – particularly in the early stages of development of the business, when planning even one year ahead counts as long term. Small firms are essentially focused on short-term plans and goals with survival as the first priority. Consequently they look to the equally short-term policies that will enable them to meet the short-term goals. Only when they have achieved some measure of stability and security can they start to look at longer-term planning and investment, staff development and training etc.

How much detail should the business plan contain?

The answer to this question will very much depend on the type of business for which the plan is being prepared. For example, the self-employed window cleaner with no overheads or equipment apart from a car, ladders, bucket, chamois and scraper will have quite simple requirements – in fact the biggest problem will probably be in planning where to get the clean water from on each part of his daily round. In comparison, someone setting up a wholesale or manufacturing business, as a hotelier, as an import/export agent or as a specialist holiday tour operator; where longer-term capital funding is required or where specific and possibly complex legislation applies, may have quite a detailed business plan.

Some self-employed people who have no need of external funding simply do not bother to prepare business plans. Others working on a part-time basis may have a very simple plan; their income may be regarded as a bonus to pay for holidays or luxuries because they may not depend on that particular activity for their main source of income or survival, e.g. part-time hairdressers, beauticians, or therapists who have a working partner, or those who have a regular day job. In reality no prescriptions can be made about the size and content of any particular business plan, as it will depend on the personal circumstances and resources of the owner-manager, the borrowing requirements needed for the business and the size, complexity and operating activity of the proposed business itself. The content and layout of the business plan will be considered in more detail in Chapter 2

References

Barclays Bank Small Business Review (1998). Training: the key to success. May. Barclays Bank plc.

Lloyds [TSB] Bank plc (1998). *Customer Information Booklet: Your Business Plan.* Lloyds Bank plc

Midland Bank plc (HSBC) (1999). *Customer Information Booklet: Starting a Business.* Midland Bank plc.

NatWest Bank and Durham University Business School (1995). *Start-up Guide.* NatWest Bank plc.

Small Firms Enterprise Development Initiative (1998). Newsletter.

Welch, B. (1995). *Developing Managers for the Smaller Business: A Report on Training and Development Needs.* Institute of Management and University of Cambridge, p. 3.

Further reading

Burns, P. and Dewhurst, J. (1996). *Small Business and Entrepreneurship.* Macmillan.

Stokes, D. (1998). *Small Business Management: A Case Study Approach.* Letts.

Chapter 2 The structure of the business plan

Chapter 2
Chapter 2

In Chapter 1 we examined the reasons and justification for preparing and using business plans, both for new and established enterprises. This chapter examines the ways in which business plans are presented, and suggests a basic structure which would be acceptable to most potential banks or financiers, in order to give the proposer of the plan plenty of flexibility in its content and presentation. This basic structure will also facilitate an efficient way of meeting the evidence requirements of the National Vocational Qualification (NVQ) Level 3 Business Planning qualification.

What format should the business plan take?

There are a multitude of 'ideal' business plans around, any or all of which will do the job for which they were designed, some better than others. Each of the major clearing banks have their own version available to potential business customers in disk or paper format, along with explanatory notes to assist completion. Other formats are available from Training and Enterprise Councils (TECs), Local Enterprise Agencies (LEAs) or from the plethora of 'Start your own business' books which abound on the shelves of most town-centre bookshops. Most of these business plans ask a range of specific questions, provide a specific amount of space for the specific answers required and specific pro forma spreadsheets with specific headings – this is where the problems start!

Probably the most common single feature that most new start-up businesses share is the very fact that they are all different from each other; and the one feature which standardized business plans with their specific questions cannot accommodate is that same disparity and uniqueness that pervades those new firms.

One of the biggest problems of standardized business plans is that they tend to restrict individual expression because they focus on factors of commonality between firms, rather than encouraging them to focus on the factors which make them different or unique from their rivals. No one should doubt or underestimate the value and use of a good budgetary plan and cash flow forecast to monitor the progress of a business, but even the finest of these will not help to sell the firm's products or services.

Not only do standardized business plan formats tend to restrict the expression of individual flair and ingenuity, by virtue of the fact that they must also accommodate a range of differing business structures they inevitably prove onerous for some business prospects and inadequate for others. For the individual who simply wants to operate, for example, as a self-employed window cleaner with a regular round and whose customers tend to pay cash on the spot, the contents of the average standardized business plan are largely superfluous as the range of business skills and the start-up capital needed to operate the business are quite modest. In comparison, in order to set up a limited company operating a chain of cyber-cafes, most standardized business plan formats would probably be inadequate. Such an enterprise would need to consider preparing budgets on a multiple location basis, and consolidating these into an overall working budget and cash flow forecast. The range of technological, management and staff supervision skills needed by the proprietors would be more extensive than in the one-man-band situation, and the finance and resources required to establish the business would equally, be much more substantial.

13

The following proposed layout for the business plan has been designed to cover the assessment and underpinning knowledge requirements of the NVQ 3 Business Planning, and the Institute of Management (IoM) Certificate in Management (Business Start-up) programmes, At the same time, it has also been designed to be sufficiently flexible to accommodate the comprehensive range of aspects which have to be addressed when approaching a bank or other financial institution for funding for the business proposal. It is by no means intended as being the one and only suitable layout to meet these purposes, but should be seen as a framework around which potential owner-managers can construct their own individual business plans by adding further material, or by omitting certain sections as may be appropriate to the size and type of business which they are planning to operate.

The layout of the business plan

Section 1 The business idea

1.1 The type of business proposed and services to be offered

This consists of a simple statement that acts as an introduction to the business plan. For example: 'I am proposing to work as a self-employed complementary therapist providing a range of treatments to my clients including aromatherapy, reflexology, reiki and holistic massage. I am qualified as a practitioner, and experienced in each of these areas, and having worked in a health clinic for the past two years, I am ready now to branch out on my own.' This statement shows in clear and simple terms, the type of work envisaged, the employment status of the owner, the range of services that will be offered and why the owner has chosen to do it.

1.2 Method of operation

This section describes briefly the way in which the business will be operated, to provide the reader (or potential financier) with an overview of how the business will operate. Taking up the previous example: 'I shall be operating as a sole-trader, working primarily from a dedicated treatment room in my home, which has been converted from a spare downstairs study. In the case of a few of my clients who are less mobile than others, I shall be visiting them in their homes to carry out their treatments.'

At this stage it is not necessary to go into great detail as the method of operation, and the reasons for its selection, will be considered later in the business plan. Again, the idea is to provide the potential financier with a preliminary insight into how the business will operate, and to describe the framework or structure of the proposed business in order to create an overall picture in the reader's mind. Once the reader has a basic understanding of your proposal, you can progress to add the details at a later stage, by which time the reader will have formed questions in his or her mind that those details will answer.

1.3 Location and operating area

You will need to explain the geographical base and catchment area from which you expect your customers to come. For some businesses, such as a mail order outlet, this is a simple matter: 'I shall be based in Rotherham, but my mail order customers will be spread throughout the United Kingdom' or, in the case of our complementary therapist, 'I shall be based in my hometown of Maidstone, and most of my customers will come from the surrounding towns and villages within a ten-mile radius of the town. The clients whom I visit will mostly live within five miles of my home'.

1.4 Outline of market and customers

This is where you provide a general outline of the type of customers who will be interested in your goods or services. Remember, at this stage an outline is all that is needed, as a more detailed analysis of your marketplace will be given in the marketing section of the business plan. For our mail order supplier: 'The customers will comprise mainly male teenagers and single adults who either belong to model aircraft clubs, or who build model aircraft as a hobby.' For our therapist they might consist of: 'Affluent middle-aged housewives, prosperous businesswomen or wealthy widows who feel the need relaxation to relieve stress and tension', or perhaps 'A cross-section of people with physical or muscular problems for which the more conventional methods of treatments have proved inadequate.'

1.5 Statement of viability

This is the initial assertion of the proposer's belief in the viability of the business, giving a summary explanation of why he or she thinks that the business will succeed. For our mail order supplier this might be the fact that 'There is currently no other supplier in the UK who is importing and distributing this particular brand of model aircraft from Japan'. For our therapist it might be that 'I already have a regular customer base on which to build, which keeps me occupied for three days per week, and I have a waiting list of twenty other clients as a result of word-of-mouth recommendation'.

Section 2 The proprietors of the business

In this section we name and describe the proprietors or the key people who will be involved in setting up and running the business, along with their respective skills and abilities which will contribute towards its success. These people may not be one and the same, as the owners may have identified others who have key skills or abilities necessary to the business but who will be employees of those owners; however, they will still be important, if not essential, to the potential success of the business.

2.1 Details of key personnel

In the case of a one-person business, this could comprise a quite simple curriculum vitae and personal profile of the business operator. However, in the case of a partnership or limited company there may be a number of key personnel involved and the role and background of each of which will need to be described in detail.

At the same time, in the case of business proposals involving a number of partners, directors or key personnel, this is the stage at which the management structure of the organization can be outlined in the form of an organization chart that specifies the respective positions and responsibilities of the key staff.

Having presented an organization chart, for each of the proprietors or key personnel shown on the chart you should then provide:

1   A curriculum vitae (ideally one page only) detailing your personal information, i.e. nationality, date and place of birth, marital status, family details, etc. It should also list your current and any ongoing qualifications or professional memberships which you expect to complete in the near future. It should summarize your career history, starting with your latest employment and working backwards, and identifying any training or experience relevant to the current business proposal. Finally, it should mention any hobbies or non-working activities or

interests which may enhance your personal profile, e.g. school governor, club secretary or treasurer, charitable activities, publications, etc.

2 A personal profile in which you describe yourself, your motivations, any past experiences which have had a major influence on your lifestyle or your career, and your personal ambitions and plans or long-term objectives for the future. It may also contain reference to any personal circumstances or family or social commitments which may influence or be of relevance to your business proposal. For example, you may have a family to support, or perhaps children with special educational needs. Alternatively, you may be in the fortunate position where you already have some alternative form of income, such as a working partner or a pension, so that you do not have to rely only on the income from your proposed business.

2.3 Your reasons for the choice of business .

In this section you should explain in more detail the various occurrences or motivating factors which have caused you to develop your plans to run your own business. In some cases this may be the result of redundancy forcing a change of direction – some people yearn for years to be their own boss, but it is only the shock and the insecurity of unemployment which forces them to take the risk. In other cases it may be as a result of an opportunity which has presented itself, offering the chance to fulfil a long-standing personal ideal or ambition, e.g. a lucrative hobby gradually expands to the extent that it finally becomes viable as a full-time business. Here the primary motivation is often one of personal satisfaction rather than financial security.

2.4 Personal skills and experience relevant to the proposed
business

This is where you can describe the various skills that you already possess or that you are currently working towards, and which you would typically evidence by certificates of qualification or references from previous employers. The important thing to remember is that it is not just certificated skills that are important. To a bank manager or prospective financier it is not only the academic (or vocational) qualifications that are taken into consideration, it is relevant previous experience that also counts. Very often, previous experience, e.g. in book-keeping, cash-management, credit-control, budgetary planning etc., is as important to a potential financier as the technical knowledge of the potential entrepreneur. This is why it is important to dredge your memory, to think back across your past working life to identify all possible experience which might be relevant to the business proposal. It is amazing how many people assume they have no prior knowledge or experience of business and yet, when asked, can describe previous jobs which involved the development and use of business skills (such as cash handling or stock control) without actually realizing that this knowledge, acquired by experience, is now relevant to their prospective business.

2.5 Appraisal of available skills, and identified
development needs

This subsection of the business plan constitutes the skills audit and skills gap analysis, and asks four key questions:

1   What skills are needed in order to achieve efficient and profitable operation of the new business? These may be technical skills or expertise such as trade or professional qualifications, business skills such as book-keeping or credit control expertise, or management experience such

as staff supervision or production planning. The important thing is to list the full range of potential skills that will certainly or might possibly be needed. Ideally this should be carried out in conjunction with someone who has experience either of the type of business activity that you are proposing and who, preferably, has past experience of running such a business. An objective opinion can be a most valuable asset, particularly if that opinion can help you to take a realistic view of your own capabilities.

2   What skills or experience have I (or my staff) accrued to date or am in the process of developing? The key to answering this question is total honesty and objectivity. Since the mid-1990s the lending banks have increasingly acknowledged the importance of self-assessment within their own standardized business plans by questioning the potential borrower's capacity for the demands of self-employment. There are various methods and techniques of self-assessment, some of which will be considered in more detail in Chapter 4.

3   What gaps or differences currently exist between the skills needed and the skills available? Having assessed the skills requirements of the business, and those available from existing or potential staff, it is necessary to define the gaps. This is the process of skills gap analysis which is designed to identify potential development areas for existing staff or other areas where new staff skills may need to be brought in or recruited. Again it is important to be totally honest and objective in identifying any gaps in skills and experience. In the face of financial or operational pressures of running a small business it is all too easy to overestimate your own capabilities, or those of your staff, or to underestimate the full range of skills which might be required in order for the business to succeed and grow.

4   How will we bridge the gap? There are two main options here: either to train and develop your own skills and/or those of existing staff, or to import (i.e. recruit) new staff who possess those essential skills, assuming, of course, that such staff are available locally. When working capital is tight, the reaction of most small businesses is to make do and mend, i.e. to do nothing. If the business cannot afford new staff, then ideally it should provide training for current staff, but with a vast majority of small firms the tendency is to skimp on investment in training. Training is often regarded as a luxury which cannot be afforded. Small firms have a fundamentally different attitude to training compared with their larger counterparts which treat training as a long-term investment. In contrast, small firms look for short-term benefits that will offer immediate measurable returns on their investment. Such training needs to be provided at low cost and convenient times so as not to lose productive working time. For most small firms, unless staff training can meet these short-term needs, it is unlikely to take place at all.

Section 3 The resources required

Before any attempt can be made at financial planning, it is essential to identify the capital investment requirements of the business (premises, transport, plant and equipment), other resources required (personnel, raw materials, consumables etc.) and the reasons why they are all needed. The process of identifying and listing them will also assist the potential owner-manager to distinguish between those resources which are desirable and those which are essential. It is surprising how many resources initially perceived as being 'essential' suddenly become regarded as luxury items when the full cost is identified, especially if the money needed to buy them has to be borrowed at high interest rates.

3.1 Inventory of required plant, equipment and materials

This is a list of all the necessary machinery, equipment and materials which might be needed to start up the business, including not just essential production equipment, but also the administrative systems (computers, office furniture), ancillary furniture and fittings (burglar alarms, safes, chairs, tables, toilets, fire extinguishers), raw materials, consumables, etc. It is only when the list is complete, and costs have started to be allocated to the various items on the list, that questions start to be asked about the necessity for individual items: 'Do I really need a Rembrandt on the wall of the executive toilet?' or, on a more practical level, 'Does the business really need two computers, or can I make do with one for the first few months?'

Once the list has been compiled costs can be allocated to each item, and a differentiation made between essential items and those that are nice to have if we can afford them. These costs need to be carefully researched with potential suppliers as they must be realistic and accurate in order to feed into the budgetary planning process. Without an accurate basis for calculating expenditure, the whole budgeting process becomes a waste of time as there is no credible or realistic basis against which subsequent expenditure and performance can be measured.

3.2 Schedule of available resources

Many people who are starting a new business have already had some partial involvement in their trade or activity, and may perhaps possess some of the resources needed to start the business. For example, if equipment has been progressively acquired whilst working on a part-time basis, the additional resources needed to turn the business into a full-time activity may not be too great. It is important, therefore, to be able to list any resources which are already available, and to put a value on these, as they will constitute part of the business owner's capital. Bank managers are always reluctant to lend money unless they can see a corresponding investment on the part of the borrower. Whilst the person setting up the business may not have a lot of spare cash to invest, the possession of equipment, materials, a car or van, or the goodwill of an existing customer base, can form part of their equity in the business, and often a very significant part. Again, it is important for the purpose of the budgetary plan to identify just how much of the cost of necessary equipment is already available, as this will reduce the net outflow of cash in the early stages.

3.3 Premises requirements, availability, necessary modifications etc.

Identifying the required premises, and finding and preparing suitable premises, is a major and time-consuming part of setting up a new business. Chapter 12 examines the various alternative forms of acquiring a suitable site, and the various contractual and legal implications involved therein. If anything, this is the aspect of establishing a new business that can have the single biggest impact (usually in terms of delay) on the commencement of a new venture, as so many of the factors are beyond the control of the owner, particularly when solicitors and town planners become involved, and more so when they decide to go on holiday, invariably one after the other. Obtaining approval for change of use or for modifications to premises can often add months to the start-up timetable.

3.4 Transport requirements

For any new business, transport is a major item of medium to long-term investment and, so, it is of paramount importance to ensure that any transport which is used or acquired will be both suitable and adequate during the lifetime for which it has been purchased. It is no good taking out a four-year hire purchase agreement on a small van if that van is likely to be too small for the needs of the business within twelve to eighteen months. So, not only must we ask the question 'What do I need right now?' but also 'Will the same thing still be suitable in a few months time?'

Finding the right vehicle will involve a number of considerations. For example:

- Is it to be used for sales and/or deliveries?

- What physical dimensions are needed or what payload is required?

- Who will drive it? Does the driver need a Heavy Goods or Public Service Licence?

- Will it incur high mileage usage and, if so, what is most economical, petrol or diesel?

- Should I buy a new or second-hand vehicle, and can I really afford a new vehicle?

- How easy is it to load and unload?

- What are the expected maintenance and running costs?

- Does it create the right image for my business?

The answers to these questions will largely determine the choice of suitable transport and the appropriate method of purchase or acquisition. Again, this information will feed into the budgetary plans and cash flow forecasts for the business.

3.5 Personnel requirements

This section will be determined to a great extent by the information gathered in the skills gap analysis in subsection 2.5 of the business plan; but the skills gap analysis will only identify the range of skills in deficit, and not the numbers of individuals needed to perform each role. Assessment of the personnel and staffing needs of the business reflects not just the range of skills needed to operate the business, but also the numbers of individuals required to work within the business. There may be a need for one person with supervisory management skills, but several with identical basic production skills to do the same job as each other, under the watchful eye of that supervisor. The numbers of each type of worker, and the associated costs of employing these must be identified in order to be fed into the budgetary plan.

3.6 Insurance requirements

The precise insurance policy requirements of the business will depend on the type of business which is proposed. As a very minimum, the owners will need to consider public liability insurance; as well as cover for theft or damage to equipment, fixtures and fittings, and possibly stock or goods in transit. If any staff are employed, albeit just a part-time cleaner, it is a legal requirement to take out employer's liability cover against accident or injury to employees. These and other insurance options are examined in more detail in Chapter 13.

Section 4 Financial plans

4.1 Budgetary plans and cash flow forecasts

For the very small business which deals largely in cash, and neither gives credit to its customers nor receives credit from its suppliers, the budgetary plan and cash flow forecast may be one and the same. For larger businesses, where credit is given or received, it will be necessary to differentiate between the two. In the eyes of the bank manager or potential financier, these are the two key documents on which much of the assessment of the viability of a potential new business are based. As such, it is important to get them right.

The budgetary plan attempts to forecast all items of income and expenditure, and details them according to when the sale is invoiced, or when the stock, goods or services are received and a financial commitment is incurred. As such it can be used to assist in the forecasting of potential sales turnover and profits, and the forecast figures can be used as a basis against which actual financial performance (income and expenditure, profit margins, etc.) can be compared.

The cash flow forecast is basically similar in structure to the budgetary plan, but is modified to take into account delays in receiving money from customers and paying money to suppliers, owing to the giving and receipt of credit. So, although the budgetary plan may show a piece of equipment as being purchased in January, payment of that invoice may not be made until a month later. Similarly, goods sold to a customer and invoiced in January may not be paid for until February or March, and in the meantime, the money due for those goods is inaccessible. A company can be making a healthy profit in budgetary terms, but can have an appalling cash flow problem due to late payment for its goods or services, which might interfere with its ability to continue trading.

4.2 Explanation of the basis for planned budgets

This section acts as a narrative explanation to the figures that appear in the budgetary plan, for example, how sales income has been forecast or why the business has used hire purchase rather than leasing to finance its vehicles. It may also outline the basis for loan interest or repayment terms, or reasons for fluctuations in levels of trading activity.

Similarly, the narrative will explain the basis for credit terms given to customers and received from its suppliers, and the impact this has on cash flow and working capital. The cash flow forecast may also indicate any overdraft requirements, or longer-term borrowing needs.

4.3 Breakeven analysis and profit forecast

It is a fundamental requirement of any business to be able to identify its breakeven level, i.e. the point at which its sales are generating sufficient contribution (surplus income) to cover both the cost of sales and the cost of overheads of the business. It is equally important that the business should be aware of its profit margins (and mark-up) so that it is able to forecast its expected profits from its anticipated sales turnover. Like the budgetary plans, this information will be an item of key interest to any bank manager or prospective financier as, without an identified profit from its trading activities, the business will be unable to repay any money which it has borrowed from them. This is a critical aspect of the assessment of the viability of any new small business as far as the banks are concerned – it just seems a shame that they did not apply the same degree of discretion when providing multimillion pound loans to certain Third World and South American countries in the 1980s, only to have them written off as bad debt a few years later. Unfortunately, the laws of bankruptcy that apply to small firms, are not so easily applied to international governments. Overseas losses on investments by the banks have resulted in cash shortages at home, restricting the money available to the owners of small firms and making it harder to raise finance. The end result is that it is imperative for the small business owner to be able to demonstrate a potential profit to its investors or financiers.

4.4 *Value of available capital and resources*

The capital which the owners of a business put into their enterprise does not just have to be in the form of hard cash. It can also consist of premises, vehicles, equipment, materials, saleable stock, or even goodwill in the form of an established customer base. In some cases, the capital may comprise a second mortgage, a charge on property as security or a personal guarantee offered against a loan. The important factor is that whatever form the capital takes, it should be measurable, and have a tangible value to demonstrate what the investor is putting into the business. Not surprisingly, bank managers are reluctant to lend money to anyone who is not prepared to back the venture themselves.

4.5 *Further finance required and potential sources of funds*

It is rare for a new small business to have all the available finance required to start it up and survive the first few months, let alone to expand itself once established. It is usually necessary at some stage to look for some form of external finance, even if that is just a short-term overdraft. Lenders will normally expect any business borrower to be investing a similar sum to that which they are asking to borrow, in order to verify their own commitment to the venture, except of course when the loan is secured against an asset such as a house or other property. Even then, although larger sums may be available, in practice the bankers' rule of thumb is that the value of the security should be roughly double that of the sum borrowed.

The various options for raising finance are considered in Chapters 6 and 8, and the appropriate options and sources of finance should be identified and described within the financial requirements section of the business plan.

4.6 Chosen sources of finance and reasons for choice

Having examined the various potential sources of finance, the business plan should identify the chosen sources, i.e. those that are most appropriate to both the owner-managers, and the type of business itself. Some firms may choose longer-term secured loans at lower rates of interest, to ease cash flow in the earlier years. Others may only need short-term initial financing, in which case the higher interest overdraft facility may be more suitable, where interest is only paid when the overdraft facility is in use.

Whatever the choice, it is necessary to describe the chosen option and the reasons for its selection over and above the alternatives. For the NVQ candidate who is preparing a business plan, the justified rejection of certain options is as much a demonstration of competence as making the choice and explaining the chosen option itself.

Section 5 Marketing

After the financial plans, it is the marketing aspects of the proposed new business which will be of greatest interest to any financier or potential investor. The marketing section of the business plan will analyse the market sector in which the business plans to operate, and the problems or barriers which might be encountered in trying to break into that market. It will then proceed to define a marketing policy which should facilitate entry and generate sales for the business.

5.1 Target market and operational area

It is important that the budding entrepreneur should have a clear idea of the market for his or her goods or services, and the physical or geographical areas in which the business will operate. This was briefly mentioned earlier in the introduction to the business plan (subsections 1.3 and 1.4). Using the same example of the mail order business, the overall market is in which the business plans to operate is that of model-makers or hobbyists, but within that market the owner is focusing on a particular sector, in this case model aircraft. This is in itself quite a broad sector with plenty of competition, and for that reason the owner has decided to focus on a specific subsector, i.e. the supply of a particular brand of Japanese model aircraft which is currently hard to obtain in this country. The specialized nature of the product means that there is likely to be insufficient trade within the geographical vicinity to make the business viable, so the owner has decided to extend the range of potential customers across the whole country by offering the product for sale by mail order.

5.2 Market research – completed and planned

In this section we investigate and analyse the particular market sector in which the proposed business expects to be operating. We must ask questions about the nature and size of the market, how easy is it to enter the market, who are the other operators within the market, and how do their products and prices etc. compare with our own. This is the process of market research, and any potential lender or investor will ask two key questions about this topic: 'What market research has been carried out to date?' and 'What other market research must be carried out before the business can be launched?' In order for any potential lender or investor to have confidence in the prospects of the business venture, it will be necessary to demonstrate that these questions have been addressed and answered in a competent and comprehensive manner, and to present the results of the research in a clear and comprehensible fashion. The process of market research is examined in more detail in Chapter 9.

5.3 Identification of any special market influences

Some markets, by virtue of their nature, are subject to specific trends, patterns or influences. The majority of postcards are sold during the summer holiday season, whilst Christmas cards tend to sell at the end of the year. The cash receipts for holiday companies follow a definite pattern, with deposits for bookings taken at the beginning of the year, followed by short peaks in trade at Easter and Whitsun, and with the bulk of sales income being received during June, July and August, then tailing off in September. The pattern is well established and recognized, and cash flow can be planned accordingly. The biggest potential disruption that can occur (apart from a war) is prolonged bad weather, and that is one factor which we cannot forecast well in advance.

In a similar vein, the operators of any new business must also attempt to identify any seasonal influences or market characteristics which will influence levels of sales, income or performance. Very often this will only be achieved as a result of direct experience gained from within the particular market, and then often only in hindsight or as a result of analysis of sales and performance figures over a period of time. For example, when I was wholesaling beers and wines to the licensed trade in the 1980s, I identified over several years a sudden substantial drop in sales around the first weeks of February and October each year, irrespective of weather etc. In spite of recent end of month salary payments, the public were not spending their money in the pubs, and so the publicans were not buying my stock. Why not? Well, quite simply, the first weeks in February and October are the deadline dates for payment or settlement of credit card balances accrued during the summer holidays in August, or in the run up to Christmas, so disposable income was at a minimum at those times. Once the pattern had been identified, stock levels could be reduced for those particular weeks in future years in order to avoid cash being tied up in unsold stock.

Whilst it is imperative to be aware of seasonal and other influences on trading levels, actually identifying these as an outsider to the market can, in fact, be very difficult, so it is important to ask questions about these potential problems as part of the market research process. Better still, try to get some experience of working within the market, or talk to someone who has done so recently.

5.4 Analysis of competitors' products and services

This analysis can be carried out by answering a series of simple questions:

- Who are my direct competitors in the marketplace, i.e. those providing the same or very similar products or services? In the case of our complementary therapist, for example, who else is offering aromatherapy massage in the district?

- Who might be competing indirectly with me, i.e. those providing other services which are not in direct competition with me, but which might detract from my sales? For example, those offering other forms of therapy which might compete with aromatherapy.

- What prices are they charging? Are they lower, higher, or comparable with my own? Why should they differ?

- How do their services differ from mine, and is this reflected in their prices?

- What geographical areas do they cover? Do these overlap with my operating area?

- Are they operating in the same market sector as myself, and what proportion of the market do they occupy? Is there space for me within that market sector?

Obtaining this information is part of the necessary process of market research, and the questions must be answered in order to produce a convincing and realistic marketing plan.

5.5 *The marketing plan*

The marketing plan constitutes the methodology statement of the business plan – 'This is how I will sell and promote my goods or services' – and the plan is typically presented using four key headings, usually described as the four Ps:

- The *Product* is about the goods or services being offered, their purpose, quality, unique features, usefulness, appeal to the customer etc.

- The *Price* of the goods or services forms the basis for comparison with competitors. Price can be a selling feature in itself, e.g. by being less than that of competitive products or, if equal, it leads the potential customer to compare quality and uniqueness with that of the competitors' products.

- The *Place* is concerned with the outlets and distribution channels through which the product will be delivered and, again, the perceptive marketing plan will look for opportunities or gaps in the marketplace, where demand is not being met.

- *Promotion* is concerned with the ways in which the products or services will be promoted or advertised to potential customers, and how the effective use of promotional activities will lead to growth in sales and expansion of the business.

This topic will be considered in more detail in Chapter 9.

5.6 Unique features of your products or services

Although stated in the marketing plan, it is a good idea to emphasize to potential lenders or investors, those features of your products or services that distinguish them from the opposition. These can be expressed in terms of quality, competitive price, durability, value for money, fashion, practical usage or even sheer sex appeal. The important thing is that you can show that you have identified those key aspects which will help to sell your product or service in the open market, and that you are making use of that information.

5.7 Schedule of fees and charges

This is a simple list of the fees or prices which you will be charging for your goods or services. It serves as a reference point for comparison with the prices charged by your competitors, as a basis for calculating profit margins and to assist in the calculation of the sales revenues that are included in your budgetary plans and cash flow forecasts. It will no doubt be influenced by the prices that are being charged by your competitors, but it should also reflect the quality of your goods or services and any distinctive or unique features which differentiate them from the competition, and for which a premium price might be justified. The use of low prices to attract business in the short term might be a justifiable strategy, but in the longer term it is maintenance of profit margins that ensures survival. The golden rule when fixing prices is that if you sell yourself short, you will almost certainly be the loser in the long term. Competitors will either reduce their prices (and profit margins) to compete with you, or look to sell their goods or services on the basis of differential features such as those described above. Finally, remember to keep a copy of your old price lists, as these are a good point of reference should the Inland Revenue start to query the profit margins you have been achieving.

5.8 Samples of advertising materials, leaflets, business cards etc.

It is always a good idea to include some samples of advertising materials such as business cards, newspaper adverts or leaflets within the business plan, although these need to have been produced to a professional standard and quality, otherwise they could well do your case more harm than good. With the wide-spread availability of computers and desktop publishing programs, most people should be able to produce a basic design of advertising material to illustrate their ideas for advertising and promotion.

5.9 Statement of quality standards and policy

This is a formal statement of the quality standards for the goods and services which are being provided, as well as for the behavioural standards of the staff which are supplying them. The statements constitute a simple description of the operating standards against which the business can be visibly measured. For example, an extract from the standards used by a wedding caterer:

- All staff will be smartly dressed at all times, and will present a friendly, smiling, and caring attitude to the customers.

- All staff involved with the preparation of food will possess a Basic Food Hygiene Certificate, and will adhere to the standards of hygiene required to comply with environmental health legislation.

- All food will be prepared on site no more than one hour before the time of serving, and covered to protect it from contamination. All food will be stored at the appropriate cold temperatures prior to preparation and before it is served.

These are just a few simple examples, but they demonstrate not just the need to comply with relevant legislation, but the emphasis on providing quality products and services to the customer, as well as the standards which the customers can expect to experience from the supplier.

Section 6 The implementation of the proposals

Having planned the financial and marketing aspects of the business, this section of the business plan focuses on the way in which the business will operate and the timetable for implementing the proposals.

6.1 Chosen means of operation and justification for choice

Here, we are identifying the legal status of the business, e.g. as a sole trader, a partnership or as a limited company, and the explanation and justification of that particular choice. The chosen method of operation may also be linked to any personal parameters, influences or ambitions that may have been identified in subsection 2.3 of the business plan.

6.2 Relevant legislation

It is important to identify any key areas of legislation which may have an impact on the business. This section should comprise a brief list which identifies the relevant legislation, accompanied by an explanation of its relevance to the business. NVQ candidates should also remember that where legislation is concerned, competence can equally be claimed where explanation is given for certain items of legislation which are not relevant to the business or its operating procedures. For example: 'I do not require planning to operate my business from my premises as there is no change of use involved, as the site already has planning consent for commercial use. However, I shall need building regulations approval to carry out modifications to the external drainage system.'

6.3 Timetable and phasing of business start-up

The budgetary plans will have identified the expected start of trading, but for many new firms there may be a lead time before trading can actually commence, e.g. where planning permission is required or where premises have to be modified. This is usually a time of net expenditure which can inevitably result in a drastic drain on available cash. It is important that realistic lead times are identified, and contingency plans made if there is any possibility of prolonged delays.

6.4 Key stages of implementation

These will vary from business to business, but they might include factors such as dates for acquiring premises, delivery of stocks or raw materials, the commencement of trading, approval of available loans or finance, key review dates or the start of an advertising campaign. The question 'What makes them key stages?' invariably invokes the answer 'If certain events are not completed by those key dates, then there could be subsequent delays in the overall implementation of the business proposal'. For example: in order to open a shop on a certain date, the shop-fitting must be completed at least three days before the opening and stock must be ordered at least three weeks before that date. A delay in receiving financial approval could mean that there is no money available to pay for the new stock on the date by which it must be ordered, so the opening date would need to be postponed.

Section 7 Monitoring and control systems

It is pointless setting out detailed budgetary plans and cash flow forecasts, or establishing and publishing statements of quality standards for a business, if the achievement of those financial plans and quality standards cannot be objectively assessed or measured. It is necessary, therefore, to have some mechanisms in place to carry out the monitoring process.

7.1 Plans for monitoring the quality of goods and services

Some methods of monitoring will be determined by legislation or by industry standards, e.g. the safe temperatures at which food can be stored, the types of thermometers to be used and the records which must be used to ensure safe storage. Others will need to be designed for the specific goods or services which the business is offering, such as the use of customer feedback questionnaires, the monitoring of the frequency of complaints or the return of unsatisfactory goods. Customer turnover or retention rates can also act as a yardstick to monitor levels of satisfaction. This subsection requires you to answer the question 'How will I ensure that my goods or services meet the necessary quality standards?' and to describe or give examples of suitable methods.

7.2 Budgetary control

Regular monitoring of planned levels of income and expenditure in comparison with the levels which are actually being achieved, is imperative if you are to keep control of the finances of the business. Any discrepancies which arise as a result of the comparison of actual and planned figures should immediately act as an alarm system, prompting questions as to the cause of the discrepancies and the actions necessary to remedy the situation. Monitoring should be carried out at least once a month, and as close as possible to the end of the previous month so that precious time is not wasted if problems do occur. It is surprising how many small firms do not realize that they have financial problems until they get their books back from their accountant three months after the end of their financial year, by which time they may already have lost too much money for the business to be able to recover or survive.

7.3 Financial control systems

Alongside the budgetary control system it is necessary to have a more basic set of day-to-day financial controls. A good double-entry book-keeping system should be maintained, using income and expenditure headings that correspond to the budget headings. The accounts should be kept up to date on a daily, or at least weekly, basis so that the cash and bank balances shown therein can be checked or reconciled against actual petty cash and bank statements. If credit is given or received it will also be necessary to maintain customer accounts and generate regular statements, particularly for money owed to the business. The aged debtors analysis will show the sums owing to the business and the length of time each has been outstanding, so that action can be taken promptly when payments are overdue.

7.4 Customer records

All businesses need to keep data and records of their customers, and if this is held on computer the information may be subject to the rules of the Data Protection Act. In addition to basic names, addresses and telephone numbers, the records may cover sales volumes of various products, financial transactions and payments, terms and conditions of contracts of supply etc. In some cases, such as the complementary therapist, the information may be much more personal, with details of medical conditions, treatments etc., and where client confidentiality is a major consideration.

A number of questions arise which will need to be answered: what records will your business need to hold and why? Are these records confidential? How will they be stored and who will be able to, access them? How often will they be updated? How secure is the method of storage?

7.5 Feedback from customers

In order to monitor the standards and quality of your goods and services, you will almost certainly have to design some means of obtaining customer feedback. The obvious way to do this is by asking your customers to complete questionnaires, or by interviewing selected samples of customers at regular intervals. Even then, it is sometimes hard to ensure that they are being totally honest and objective rather than being polite. It is often necessary, therefore, to examine other ways of assessing your performance or of verifying the usefulness of the feedback you have been given. One way is to ask new customers how they have found out about you, e.g. via sales activity or advertisements or as a result of recommendation from other existing customers. The frequency of recommendations will be a basic means of determining levels of customer satisfaction. Alternatively, if you are in the type of business which involves trading with customers on a regular basis, it may be more valuable to monitor rates of customer turnover. There will always be some degree of natural wastage as people move, retire or even die, but the retention of customers and their subsequent loyalty to your business can provide a firm indication of the quality of your goods or services or, in some cases, the apparent lack of it.

7.6 How will the success of the business will be measured?

The obvious answer to this question is simple – by how much profit the business is making. But the achievement of the business can be measured in more ways than that, for example, by:

- Assessing the quality of goods or services as described in customer feedback, against established quality standards.

- Measuring rates of growth of the business as a whole, or the growth of its various constituent parts, in comparison with previous years, or forecast figures.

- Comparing actual with planned income and expenditure for each period.

- Measuring customer retention rates with past performance.

- Assessing growth of sales in relation to promotional activities and expenditure.

- Comparing the relative sales levels of individual goods or services.

- Monitoring profit margins by product or service.

- Monitoring overall cash profit, and profit margins, to ensure solvency.

- Analysis of aged debtors and creditors, payment terms etc., to ensure liquidity.

It is important to identify which of these alternatives, or combinations thereof, are appropriate to your type of business and to define the ways in which you will use them to measure your success.

Section 8 Summary

This is a final section in which the reasons for the belief in the viability and potential success of the business are summarized and reaffirmed. This should take the form of a list of key points, each stating a reason and a corresponding justification for the anticipated success of the business. For example, 'I believe that the business will be profitable for the following reasons:

1 I already have a core of regular customers who are satisfied with the products and services that I offer, along with a waiting list of potential clients.

2 I currently have no direct competitors within a twenty-mile radius of my operating area, and I am not aware of any others who are planning to work in my locality.

3 I have adequate finance and working capital to buy all necessary plant and equipment, and sufficient working capital to finance the first twelve months of trading, even without expanding my current turnover.

4 I have sufficient collateral in my own home to raise any necessary finance for expansion, even though I fully expect growth of my business to be financed from its own profits.

5 I have all the necessary skills and experience to successfully operate the business, along with two experienced and reliable staff who can back me up during holidays or in the event of illness. My domestic partner is an experienced and qualified book-keeper, and my brother is a solicitor.

6 I have a low-rent, long-term lease on premises which are adequate both for current output and foreseeable growth.'

It sounds just like heaven, does it not? If only all business start-ups were that straightforward!

Further reading

Blackwell, E. (1998). *How to Prepare a Business Plan*. Kogan Page.
Burns, P. and Dewhurst, J. (1996). *Small Business and Entrepreneurship*. Macmillan.
Stokes, D. (1998). *Small Business Management: A Case Study Approach*. Letts.
Writing a Business Plan. Institute of Management Checklist No. 021.

Chapter 3 The business idea

Chapter 3
Chapter 3

The objective of this chapter is to help the new or prospective owner-manager to make a realistic, and hopefully objective, assessment of the viability of the proposed or new business venture. This chapter also relates to Unit A1 of NVQ Level 3 Business Planning, 'Assess the potential of the proposed Business', which in Element A1.1 is concerned with describing the business, how it will operate, and the goods and services it will be offering. Element A1.2 carries out an initial review of the marketplace and Element A1.3 encourages the evaluation of the likely success of the business. Whether or not the reader is pursuing the NVQ qualification, each of these three exercises offers a great deal of value in its own right in setting the scene for the ensuing parts of the business plan.

The business idea section of the business plan, the structure of which was outlined in the previous chapter, plays a key role in introducing the proposed venture to any banker or potential investor. It is intended primarily as an overview of the business plan, and as such, it does not have to be crammed full of detail – that can follow later – but it must be regarded as a principal opportunity for promoting and selling your business. The fact is that, unless the introduction can provide a concise, positive and optimistic (but still realistic) summary of the business opportunity that will whet the appetite of the reader, then the chances are that any potential banker, financier or investor will simply not bother to read any further. It must, therefore, project and reflect the proposer's confidence and belief in the proposed business, and emphasize and justify that same belief. It is simply no good stating 'Well, I think that it might work', as the bank manager would be quite justified in saying 'Then come back and see me when it has'. It is important, therefore, to think positively and to use positive language throughout the business plan: you do not hope to succeed, you expect to succeed; you will do something, rather than might do it.

In my experience, most new or aspiring entrepreneurs tend to overlook two fundamental points. First, bank managers do not have unlimited funds to lend, so your proposition needs to stand out from the crowd and justify the bank manager's decision to lend to you. Second, the business plan is not just a factual document. One of the primary skills that any owner-manager needs in order to succeed, is the ability to sell their goods or services to the customers. Naturally, when a bank manager is appraising any business plan, he or she will be looking for evidence of those selling skills. So for that very reason it is important that the initial part of the business plan not only grabs their attention, but also starts to demonstrate the presence of those selling skills. Put yourself in the bank manager's shoes – if you are unable to project to the bank manager your own belief in the viability of the business, then why should he or she believe in it?

NVQ candidates who are working on Unit A1 will need to evidence the following items:

- The nature and purpose of the business, new business, purchase of existing business, franchise etc., discussed below.

- The way in which it will operate, i.e. the trading status, again examined below.

- Any legislation which will affect the business. This is examined in detail in Chapter 5.

- The intended market(s), range of products or services and the customers' needs, the potential size of the market, identifying your competitors and any potential barriers to entry into the market. These aspects are covered in detail in Chapter 9.

- Any external factors which might influence the business, e.g. economic factors.

- The financial requirements to set up and operate the business. These are examined in Chapters 6, 7, and 8.

- The management and technical skills that will be needed for the business, which are assessed in Chapter 4.

- The likely profits which will be generated by the business. This is also considered in Chapter 6.

So, having recognized that each of the above areas will be covered in more detail elsewhere in the business plan (or the NVQ portfolio), at this stage the evidence primarily comprises a statement summarizing those key points.

The purpose of the business

The very first point that must be explained is the nature of the business activities. It may well be that the business will focus on providing just one type of goods or service – a chiropodist, for example, carries out medical treatment to people's feet. However, in some cases, the central goods or service may be accompanied by a secondary line, for example, some chiropodists also carry out reflexology (foot massage) treatments.

It is important from the outset that the primary and secondary activities are clearly defined in an initial statement, so that the reader is immediately informed of the nature of the business. For example: 'I intend to set up in business as a mobile caterer specializing in private functions such as weddings and parties. Alongside the provision of food and drink for weddings,

I can also offer secondary associated services. These will include the supply of wedding cakes, licensed bars, chauffeur-driven cars, discos, flowers, and wedding photography, which I will arrange as part of a complete package for my clients and for which I will receive a percentage commission from the specialist suppliers.' In this case, the primary service of food and drink for functions is clearly stated, and the secondary income from supplementary services is also explained.

Is this a new or existing business?

This is an obvious, but still important, question to answer for the benefit of any potential financier as the answer to it will invariably raise a series of further questions:

- Is this a new business that you are setting up from scratch? If so, assuming that you have done your market research and justified the viability of the prospect, then you must identify the lead time between start-up and reaching an ongoing operating profit. This leads to the questions: 'Are your financial resources adequate to cover that period?' or 'What could possibly go wrong that might delay your trading at a profit?' and 'How would you cope with that problem?' You need, therefore, to be in a position to answer these questions if asked, and ideally your business plan should demonstrate that you have considered them.

- Are you setting up a franchised business? If so, you should be able to demonstrate the type and level of support available in the early stages from the operators of the franchise, and confirm their reputation as franchisers. How well known are the franchised products or services? Have you spoken to other franchisees to investigate their experience in the early stages? Do you have any exclusive operating area rights to protect you from neighbouring franchisees? Are you tied in to a long-term contract? Do you face any penalties if your franchise fails?

- If you are buying an established business, are you sure of its long-term viability? Is it threatened in any way by new developments in the area or by incoming competition? Will it be affected by any economic or legislative factors? Are you paying a fair price? Has your contract to buy been checked by a solicitor and the financial books examined by an accountant? Why does the vendor want to sell in the first place, and is the reason given genuine? Will you be able to make a reasonable return on the capital invested?

In the process of describing the proposed business, the reader will need to have made some basic decisions about the format of the business, e.g. whether it will be operated on a sole trader basis, as a partnership or a limited company. In doing so, the reader may also need to consider some of the legal aspects described in Chapter 5. First, however, it is worth examining the various options of trading status in more detail.

The legal format of the business

Sole trader

Being a sole trader is not simply a case of being a one-man band, as many sole traders actually employ quite a few staff – just think about some of the local builders or trades people in your vicinity. Sole trader status means that the person who owns and runs the business is solely responsible for its profits, losses, legal and statutory obligations, liabilities etc.

On the positive side, this means that the sole trader does not have to answer to anyone else (unless married!), and is solely responsible for decision-making. It is easy to start trading, as all that is necessary is to inform the local Inland Revenue office by completing a standard form which is available from the tax office, Department of Social Security or the local Customs and Excise (VAT) office. All profits are retained by the proprietor and he or she can determine the hours worked, duration of their holidays, etc. With the aid of a good accountant, they can also minimize tax liabilities, as they are taxed on the profits of the business rather than the wages or drawings taken from the business. In fact, the overall operation of the business can be quite simple.

This all sounds very attractive, but naturally there is also a downside. As well as retaining all profits, the sole trader is directly liable for all losses, without any limit to the liability. If the business folds, then creditors can pursue the sole trader's own personal assets: home, car, jewellery, savings, and all but the very basic possessions. Attachment Orders can also be made against future earnings. Unless the business is sufficiently large to employ staff, working hours can be long, holidays are often few and far between, and there is often no backup in the case of illness or accident. It can also be lonely having to make decisions without anyone with whom you can discuss issues or problems, or ask for an objective and honest opinion. Capital is also hard to raise without security, although that problem can be true of most new businesses.

Legally, unless they are subject to special registration or reporting requirements for a particular trade or industry (e.g. environmental health registration for caterers), the statutory reporting requirements are quite simple. If sales turnover is less than £15 000 per annum, then a simple three-line tax return is sufficient (sales less expenses equals profit), and above that level the sole trader need only complete the appropriate parts of the annual self-assessment form for tax purposes, profit and loss account details etc. Once sales turnover reaches £50 000 per annum then, like any other business, it is necessary to register for VAT with HM Customs and Excise, and to make the necessary quarterly returns and payments, as described in Chapter 5. Also, if employing staff, then income tax and National Insurance contributions (NIC) must be deducted from their wages or salaries under the Inland Revenue pay as you earn (PAYE) system. Sole trader accounts do not have to be audited by a chartered accountant, but all records do have to be retained for a period of six years. Profits, less legitimate business expenses and personal allowances, are taxable and every sole trader must pay Class 2 NIC, unless income is low. Class 4 NIC is also levied by the Inland Revenue according to the level of profits.

Partnerships

A partnership is a business involving two or more partners who are trading together as a single business. Typically the business relationship will be formalized under a legally constituted and legally binding partnership agreement (see Partnership Act 1890 in Chapter 5), and the Inland Revenue have to be informed when the partnership starts or is closed down.

Many people find the added security offered by a partnership to be attractive. For example, with two or more people working together, there is usually a better interaction of ideas when it comes to decision-making – two heads are better than one. There is also the mutual support available in the event of illness or accident, and to facilitate more flexible working hours and holidays. Profits are retained by the partners and, whilst shared, will often be greater than the same individuals could achieve by working separately, because of the savings gained by sharing administration and overhead costs and by using specialist skills and expertise. For example, one partner may have strong sales skills, whilst the other may have better financial and administrative abilities. A partnership may also provide an easier means of raising finance or of providing a greater sum of available finance; where, for example, available monies are pooled or security for loans is shared.

Again, however, there is a negative side to partnerships which should not be underestimated. It is often said that there is nothing like a business partnership to test a friendship, or to divide a family in two! Differences of opinion can arise over what direction the business should take, or over who is working the hardest or longest hours, or drawing the biggest income from the business. The cracks become more noticeable when the business is under financial pressure or when individual partners come under pressure from their own spouses or families. It is hard to convince your spouse that you cannot afford a holiday this year because the business needs a new van, and then to see your business partner go off to the Costa del Sol a week later.

The biggest drawback of partnerships is the personal liability of the partners for the debts of the business, that is, the 'joint and several liability' wherein each partner is liable for their own proportion of any debts plus the liability for the debt as a whole. Consider the following cases.

Case studies

A two-woman partnership is assessed for a tax liability of £2000. Partner A pays the Inland Revenue her half of the liability on time, i.e. £1000. Partner B then defaults on her share, and disappears to South America with her new toy boy. Partner A now becomes liable for B's share of £1000 as well as the money she has already paid.

This example is based on true circumstances wherein two partners running a private club got into debt with HM Customs and Excise for late payment of VAT. The bailiffs entered the premises, removed all assets and closed it down. Partner X had a heart attack and died, so partner Y declared himself voluntarily bankrupt, leaving the widow of partner X having to pay all business debts from her late husband's estate and insurance.

True, legal redress can be obtained, but the cost, aggravation and lengthy timescales involved often do not justify the effort.

The moral is to be very sure of the person or persons with whom you are going into partnership. Can you fully trust them? Are they honest? Are they reliable? Are their objectives for the business the same as yours? Do they also regard it as a long-term prospect, or is it just a 'get rich quick' idea in which they will lose interest when the going gets tough? How does their level of investment compare with your own, i.e. who is taking the most risk? Do they have any business skills or experience? What can they offer you that you cannot get by employing someone? These are just a few of the questions you may need to ask yourself before making a full commitment.

From the point of view of legal reporting, the requirements for a partnership are very similar to those for the sole trader. The same accounting returns have to be made on turnover, expenses and profits for tax purposes. The PAYE and National Insurance requirements are the same, as is the VAT threshold, which is more likely to be reached when two or more people are generating income for the business.

Limited company

Limited companies are generally regarded as being of a higher status than sole traders or partnerships. They can be purchased quite readily 'off the peg', via weekly publications such as *Dalton's Weekly* or *Exchange & Mart*. The new companies are set up en bloc up by specialist firms, offered for sale for approximately £200, and then renamed as required to start trading. Assuming there are no anticipated problems with the proposed trading name, once the company has been purchased and company officers nominated the company can start trading almost immediately. Alternatively, they can be set up very cheaply from scratch, under the proposed operating name, in about four to five weeks without much legal advice. In reality, to avoid the time delay and administration involved, it is much simpler to pay a little more for a company from a specialist supplier and then simply change the name.

The main documents required in order for the company to operate, are the Memorandum and Articles of Association which define the company's legitimate trading activities and powers to raise finance. The company must also maintain a Minute Book in which to record the share capital, issue of shares, details of company officers, minutes of annual general meetings etc. Every limited company also has a company seal which is affixed to official documents and contracts. Responsibilities and duties of company officers are established in law, and necessary statutory returns (and penalties for non-compliance) are specified by the Companies Acts.

The key difference between sole traders and partnerships, and the directors who own or manage limited companies, is that the former are self-employed but directors cannot legally be so as they are employees of the company. This is because the limited company is a 'body corporate', i.e. it has a legal existence in its own right, irrespective of the persons who own it, invest in it or manage it. Similarly, whereas self-employed sole traders and partners are taxed as individuals and pay income tax, a limited company having a corporate identity, is liable for corporation tax. It is the same corporate status that makes the liability of its owners limited. This means that unlike sole traders and partners whose liability for business debts is total, the owners, investors, shareholders etc. of a limited company are only liable for the sums which they have already invested in the company, or which they have guaranteed on its behalf. (That liability also includes the value any shares which are issued but not fully paid up.) If, therefore, the company becomes insolvent, the creditors can only pursue the assets of the company and cannot take action against the shareholders or directors, except in the case of fraud or negligence by those same persons.

On the face of things, this seems a very attractive and low-risk way of setting up a business, as the limited company approach ostensibly takes the owner one step back from potential creditors. However, things are not that simple. I heard of a retired middle manager from a water authority who had no direct experience of small firms, but who was telling a business start-up group that if they wanted to be taken seriously they must set up a limited company. This was because 'sole traders and partnerships have no real credence in the business world'. In reality this is total nonsense where new businesses are concerned, because a newly established limited company with no financial track record, and with only £100 of issued share capital, is totally unattractive.

For any start-up business the two foremost problems consist of finding the finance to get started, and then obtaining credit from suppliers to trade and expand the sales of the business. It matters not whether you are a sole trader or a limited company if you have no proven track record and no tangible assets or security to offer, in which case borrowing money or obtaining credit will be hard. This is because you will be unable to provide any necessary trade references and, in the case of limited companies, a search via Companies House will show no accounts as having been returned. Quite often, suppliers of goods to limited companies will take a harder line than that taken with sole traders, simply because they know that it is easier to recover debt from a sole trader than from the owners of a limited company. It is quite common for initial terms of supply to be based on cash with order, or cash on delivery, with credit facilities being withheld until the buyers have proven their reliability. Even then, credit may be limited to a fixed monthly maximum figure, or to payment within a fixed period of time, until a good working relationship has been established.

In terms of legal and statutory reporting requirements, owners of limited companies have more onerous obligations than their self-employed counterparts. For those with a relatively low turnover (under £2.8 million) the submission of abbreviated accounts is permissible, but for the majority, it is necessary annually to submit full audited accounts to the Registrar of Companies. The annual returns, etc. are examined in more detail in Chapter 5. In addition, as all directors are employees of the company, all staff come under PAYE and National Insurance regulations, plus the additional requirement to provide the Inland Revenue with details of all expenses for each director and higher paid member of staff. Value added tax thresholds are the same as for any other business.

In summary then, the limited company option is probably more suited to the type of business which foresees steady and continuous growth and employment of staff, whereas the smaller business which is not looking for substantial expansion would probably benefit from remaining as a partnership or sole trader status. Having said that, the government's 1999 Budget contained tax incentives to effectively encourage sole traders and small partnerships to trade as limited companies, as those are easier to monitor and control via the Registrar of Companies.

Co-operative

The fourth trading status option for smaller businesses is to become established as a co-operative or joint ownership venture, wherein the business is owned and controlled by a minimum of seven members, normally but not necessarily its own employees, as there can be non-working members. This is usually described as a 'workers co-operative' to distinguish it from the various Co-operative Retail Societies (Co-op shops) across the UK which are in effect customer-owned co-operatives. Although co-operatives are normally limited companies, they can be societies or even partnerships (the John Lewis Partnership of department stores is a good example of this) as they are regulated and registered under the Provident Societies Acts (1965–75). This means that all the business policy, assets, and profits of a co-operative are controlled by its own members (or staff) who all have equal voting rights in how the business is organized and managed. Wages are paid to staff, and surplus profits (dividends) shared between them according to their level of participation in the business. Like limited companies, registered co-operatives are classed as a 'bodies corporate' and are subject to corporation tax although, if unregistered, they are treated as partnerships with unlimited liability for the losses or debts of the business. When registered in the form of a limited company, their reporting requirements will be the same as those of normal limited companies, as will be the operation of PAYE, tax liabilities, VAT registration, etc.

Involvement in a co-operative does usually generate a high level of commitment from its members, as they are effectively working for the good of themselves as well as the co-operative and they participate in the management and decision-making processes. At times, however, this democratic process can be counterproductive, when business decisions are based on personal feelings or interest rather than sound business practice. Where co-operatives have been created as worker buyouts of failing businesses when faced with possible redundancy, the result is often the continuation of inefficient labour-intensive working methods to maintain employment for members, which can threaten its own success or survival.

The government's Co-operative Development Agency exists to advise any potential co-operatives how to set themselves up. These days, apart from special areas of mutual interest (e.g. organic farming, social or environmental interests), co-operatives are relatively uncommon, and certainly there is little or no commercial advantage to be gained from setting up as one.

External influences

It is relatively easy to identify the factors which will impact on the viability of a business from within the business itself (staff, management skills, available finance, etc.) and from the market environment (size of market, demand for goods and services, competition, etc.). However, most aspiring owner-managers find it much harder to focus on the broader influences, particularly if they are not familiar with economics or do not have a great deal of interest in politics or current affairs.

One of the most widely used methods of analysing these factors is the PESTLE analysis, which categorizes the factors under the six main headings of Political, Economic, Social, Technological, Legislative, and Environmental influences. The precise relevance of these will of courses, depend on the individual organization, its particular geographical location, and the market in which it operates; so these are best illustrated with a few examples.

Political influences

These would include such things as government policy on transport, unemployment, regional development, education and training, etc. So, for example, there may be financial incentives to locate a new business in a rural development area; or perhaps on a site close to where a new motorway junction is to be built. Foreseeable changes in policy may also present a threat, such as the heavy taxation of petrol and diesel to persuade people to use public transport. This will obviously create an ever-increasing overhead cost to any business which is involved in producing or transporting bulky goods over long distances. Can you identify any government policies which might influence or impact on the operation of your business in the near future?

Economic factors

These can take on many different aspects, and can be hard to forecast in the longer term as the international economic situation is influenced by a multitude of national policies, changes in demand, recession, inflation etc. For example, high interest rates and a steady and relatively low level of inflation in the UK has resulted in a strong pound during the late 1990s, making imports cheap but exported goods expensive, so exporting companies have noticed a general decline in sales. At the same time, financial problems within countries in the Pacific Basin made their currencies weak and their own exports cheaper to buy in the UK. Interest rates are often used as a mechanism to control inflation, but invariably also impact on rates of exchange of currency so that the combination of higher interest payments on loans coupled with falling export sales could seriously damage cash flow for a small firm. Higher interest rates can also reduce the amount of disposable income for consumers, who then focus their spending on necessities rather than luxury goods. This is not so good if you are planning to set up as a producer or importer of those same luxury goods. The question is, which of these economic influences might be relevant to your particular proposal, if not immediately, then over the next few years?

Social influences and trends

These tend to occur more slowly and are therefore a little easier to forecast than economic trends. Since the late 1970s there has been an increase in public awareness of environmental and conservation issues, and a move towards reducing waste, recycling etc. Corresponding to this, there has been a similar reaction against products which are not regarded as environmentally friendly, so producers and suppliers have had to respond to these trends and modify their goods and services accordingly. A parallel trend has been the change in attitude to healthy living, with fewer smokers, more people taking regular exercise, and a proliferation of organic foods and health products. This change in lifestyle has accompanied a change in expectations of the goods and services people buy, particularly in terms of the brand image and quality of the goods and services on offer. So how do these recent trends impact on your goods and services? Can you identify any other changes that are now, or might in future, be relevant to you?

Technological change

The first electronic calculators came on general sale in the early 1970s, with limited capacity but very expensive compared with other consumer goods. These sold for £25 each at a time when petrol was 50p per gallon, beer 20p per pint, and only large organizations could afford a computer for their accounts. Within ten years, stand-alone computers arrived, featuring a huge 10 megabytes of memory and costing as little as £5000 each! Now they cost a tenth of the price, run 500 times faster, and have 1000 times as much memory. In the 1960s and 1970s everyone spoke of the time before the end of the century when we would all be working just twenty hours per week for the same level of income. The 1990s would be the Leisure Age. In reality, technology via robotics and computers has chopped the number of people now working, and those who are working tend to work longer hours under much more pressure – particularly amongst small firms. People increasingly work from home, or away from the central business locations, using electronic communications systems. The point is that technology changed must faster and in different directions in the last twenty years of the twentieth century than had originally been forecast. Although it is virtually impossible to predict the rate or direction of change for the future, it is important that the owner-manager stays alert to the effects of possible change, and that this awareness is made apparent within the business plan.

Legislative changes

As a result of closer involvement with the European Union (EU), there have been dramatic changes in legislation in recent years. For example, the EU Social Chapter has improved the rights of both full-time and part-time employees and, in 1998, the Working Hours Directive increased the rights to paid holiday each year, and substantially reduced the maximum average working hours each week. (This is discussed further in Chapter 5.) A change in UK food hygiene regulations in 1991 forced many catering outlets to scrap and completely change their refrigeration systems. This in itself was a positive move in the public interest, but a year later the EU introduced further regulations, imposing tighter limits and additional costs to modify and change the recently bought equipment. Some of the biggest impacts on small businesses have come from the imposition of milk quotas under the EU Common Agricultural Policy, and restricted fishing quotas under the Fisheries Policy. The farmers who invested in dairy herds, and the trawler owners who took out long-term loans to buy boats, had done so in good faith assuming that there was no foreseeable short-term threat to their livelihoods. Health and safety is another area where changes in legislation can have heavy financial implications for business owners and operators.

The point about these examples is that it is important to be aware of changing legislation, and not just the changes going on within the UK. It is particularly important when you are planning to buy an existing business to check on any forthcoming legal changes that might have prompted the sale. Just before the advent of the abolition of restrictions on duty paid import of beer and wines in 1993, there was a large number of public houses up for sale in East Kent at attractive prices. Within the next two years, there was also a large number of less astute public house landlords in the same area, who were declared bankrupt as a result of a sharp decline in local trade.

Environmental issues

Some of these have already been mentioned in connection with social trends which often tend to arise as a result of philanthropy or social awareness, but there are other much more practical examples. In Chapter 5 reference is made to the impact of the Clean Air Act and the Control of Pollution Act. These are constantly being modified and standards upgraded to improve the environment. When waste disposal tipping licences were introduced in 1974 there was still a fair amount of space (primarily holes in the ground resulting from mineral extraction) available for tipping. More recently that space has been in short supply and the cost of transporting waste over longer distances has spiralled. Now the emphasis is increasingly on the reduction of use of packaging materials and the compulsory recycling of those materials in many industries. Along with the reduction of exhaust emissions, and tighter control of use and disposal of toxic materials, this is an aspect of environmental control that will inevitably expand. So how will these affect your business now, or in the future? Have you allowed for the possible increase in overhead costs within your business plan? Is your particular business likely to be subject to any other changes in environmental controls in the near future?

Further reading

Burns, P. and Dewhurst, J. (eds) (1996). *Small Business and Entrepreneurship*. Macmillan.

Clayton, P. (1998). *Law for the Small Business*. Kogan Page.

Stokes, D. (1998). *Small Business Management: A Case Study Approach*. Letts.

Williams, S. (1998). *Lloyds Bank Small Business Guide*. Penguin.

Chapter 4 Personal
Chapter 4
Chapter 4
skills and
abilities

There have been many people who in the past have nursed a secret aspiration to run their own business. For most, the prospect remains just a wishful thought. For others, something happens in their lives which presents an opportunity, perhaps an unexpected inheritance or an event which forces a change in direction, such as redundancy. But simply having the money to start a business is not enough. Even in the case of the trades person who is made redundant, possessing both the technical skills needed to work and the redundancy pay-out to start on his or her own, surviving in business requires a much wider portfolio of skills. The problems lie, first, in identifying which specific skills are most relevant to the business proposal and, second, in determining objectively whether or not these skills are available. In the event that the required skills are not currently available, then those deficient skills must either be developed or imported. The process of identifying the necessary skills and assessing their presence is called the skills audit.

The objectives of this chapter are to assist the reader in understanding how to carry out a skills audit, and to provide some practical methods of self-assessment which will assist him or her, as a potential owner-manager, to define the skills gaps which need to be filled. Following on from that, the reader will be able to define his or her own personal development plan to acquire the further skills needed to succeed in business.

This chapter also relates to Unit 2 of the NVQ Level 3 Business Planning, 'Assess your own skills and capabilities for running the business', which is concerned with four key stages:

- Objectively analysing and identifying the current and foreseeable skills needs of the business, in terms of management, administrative and technical skills, and the relative importance of these.

- Identifying your own personal goals and objectives, and accurately analysing and evaluating your own skills and resources in relation to these.

- Producing a realistic personal development plan.

- Monitoring your ongoing performance as an owner-manager, and your progress in developing new skills.

What skills does my business need to make it successful?

First, when answering this question, it is important to remember that we are not just looking at those skills needed right at this moment, but also those which will be required as the business starts to expand. As a rule of thumb, the smaller the business, the wider the range of skills that the owner-manager will need to operate the business, particularly in the early stages of its development. It is important, therefore, to draw up a skills profile for the business identifying the diverse range of expertise required:

- *Technical knowledge* of, or expertise in, the goods or services which you plan to provide, and how the customers will make use of them. From the customer's perspective, the supplier is the specialist who is expected to answer all the awkward questions.

- *Marketing skills* – to enable you to research your market, to design a marketing plan to promote and distribute your goods or services. Many owner-managers set up in business in an area with which they are already familiar and so have some basic knowledge of their market, but there is still a need to maintain objectivity, particularly when estimating market share and sales volumes.

- *Sales skills* – these are often assumed to be the same as marketing skills, but there is a distinct difference. You may have an excellent product and a market ripe to take it, but you still need the skills to persuade your customers, or your distributors, that it is your product they should be using or retailing, rather than one supplied by a competitor. In the early stages of developing your business, you may not be able to afford to pay a full-time sales person.

- *Organizational skills* – the ability to plan and organize yourself and your business, to ensure that your staff, resources, materials, finished goods etc., are in the right place at the right time. Careful planning and attention to detail enables you to make the most productive use of time and resources, and to avoid costly waste.

- *Decision-making* – the facility to analyse problems, identify and evaluate options and make objective and rational decisions.

- *Financial skills* – keeping day-to-day accounts is not necessarily the best use of the owner-manager's time; a part-time book-keeper or accountant would probably be much more cost-effective. However, it is still important for the owner to be able to understand the accounting procedures. In particular, it is essential to have a basic understanding of budgetary planning and control, in order to keep the business on track and to spot any potential problems.

- *Customer service skills* – this is not just a case of keeping the customers satisfied by providing a consistently high standard of service. For small firms one of the biggest headaches in dealing with customers is debt collection, and persuading your customers to pay their bills on time without the risk of offending them or losing their business.

- *Staff management skills* – the ability to supervise, delegate work, train and motivate staff to get the best out of them. The importance of this is often underestimated, especially by new owner-managers who have never previously been involved with managing staff. One of the hardest aspects is that of trusting the staff to get on with the job without constant close scrutiny, so that the owner can get on with the job of running the business.

- *Management of information and computer literacy skills* – the use of word-processing, databases, desktop publishing, accounting software, moving around the Internet, communication by e-mail etc.

The skills audit: what skills do you (or your staff or associates) already have?

Once you have identified the range of skills which the business will need, the next stage is to identify which of those you, as the owner-manager, already possess or those which can be provided by staff or associates. Where there is an obvious gap in the skills, you have to decide whether or not it can be filled by developing them within yourself or another person within the business. If it can, then you must consider how this is going to be achieved, e.g. by attending a training course. In some cases it may just be easier and more convenient to buy in the skills, as in the earlier example of accounts, where a part-time book-keeper employed for a few hours per week may be sufficient for the first year or two of the business. Sales skills are another good example as full-time sales staff are expensive to finance until the business becomes established, and yet without them the business will never be able to grow. Very few owner-managers can devote sufficient time to do as much selling as they really need, so the short-term answer is often a compromise, involving a part-time or commission only sales agent to supplement the owner's sales activities. Then, once the firm is established, it can look to employing permanent sales staff.

Before we can think about employing staff, we need to examine some methods of self-assessment which will assist in identifying both the skills which are present and those that are needed. There are a host of different methods of self-assessment, for example psychometric tests, learning style questionnaires etc. The examples described below have been chosen because they are easy to use, are relevant to the needs of owner-managers and provide good examples for inclusion in the business plan for presentation to the bank manager, and as evidence for NVQ portfolios.

SWOT analysis

It is becoming increasingly hard these days to find anyone who has never completed a SWOT analysis in one form or another, but its popularity is a reflection of its simplicity and usefulness. The idea is that the person making the analysis lists their own personal Strengths and Weaknesses (i.e. those factors which are a part of the person themselves) affecting the proposed business. They also examine and list the Opportunities and Threats (i.e. the external factors) which might affect the business. For example:

Strengths Sales skills, good technical product knowledge, enthusiasm.

Weaknesses No knowledge of accounts, poor computing skills.

Opportunities Offer of cheap premises, existing customer base.

Threats Lack of working capital, strong local competition.

In view of the subjective nature of a SWOT analysis, it is quite possible for people to underestimate or overestimate their personal skills and capabilities. To make the process more objective it is recommended that, when the subject has carried out their own analysis, they should get another person to complete the analysis for them and then compare the two outcomes. The SWOT analysis is a useful element to include in a business plan, and is a key evidence requirement for Unit A2 of the NVQ.

What makes a good manager?

Exercise

This exercise is designed to get the participants thinking about a host of different management skills, their relative importance or usefulness, and which of them the participants need to develop for themselves. Figure 4.1 contains a list of seventy-two 'management' skills, which cover a broad range of technical, organizational, business and interpersonal skills of the types required by the average owner-manager.

Stage 1 The participants examine the seventy-two skills, and categorizes them under three alternative headings: 'Managing yourself', 'Managing others' and 'Managing tasks'.

Stage 2 The participants identify what they regard as the ten most important skills in each of the three areas, and list them in order of priority.

Stage 3 The participants grade themselves against each of the thirty selected skills, on a scale of 1 to 5, with 5 being the highest. As a double check they can also ask a colleague or manager to grade them against the same thirty skills.

Stage 4 The participants select the two weakest skills from each category as being potential areas for self-development, and complete an action plan for developing the two skills. A sample action plan is shown in Figure 4.2.

1.	Showing enthusiasm	37.	Concentrating on the task in hand
2.	Making an impact	38.	Valuing continuous improvement
3.	Being assertive	39.	Managing change
4.	Taking responsibility	40.	Monitoring
5.	Being flexible	41.	Adapting
6.	Being objective	42.	Being proactive
7.	Able to manage under pressure	43.	Implementing
8.	Showing resilience	44.	Handling complexity
9.	Dealing with uncertainty	45.	Collating and handling information
10.	Being self-aware	46.	Thinking conceptually
11.	Valuing oneself	47.	Logical and analytical thought
12.	Being an active learner	48.	Focusing on problems
13.	Developing oneself	49.	Thinking strategically
14.	Exercising self-discipline	50.	Being creative
15.	Setting high personal standards	51.	Making judgements
16.	Showing sensitivity to others	52.	Possessing common sense
17.	Empathizing	53.	Using time efficiently
18.	Measuring performance	54.	Being decisive
19.	Listening and questioning	55.	Being consistent
20.	Influencing	56.	Treating people fairly
21.	Handling conflict well	57.	Respecting others
22.	Valuing others	58.	Avoiding waste
23.	Developing other people	59.	Being respected by others
24.	Challenging and confronting	60.	Setting clear targets and objectives
25.	Being supportive	61.	Belief in equal opportunities
26.	Being at ease with people	62.	Showing care and attention
27.	Encouraging ethical behaviour	63.	Putting people at ease
28.	Motivating people	64.	Optimizing use of resources
29.	Working effectively in teams	65.	Delegating responsibility
30.	Networking	66.	Allocating work efficiently
31.	Envisioning	67.	Managing budgets
32.	Admitting own short-comings	68.	Communicating information
33.	Seeking opinions of others	69.	Prioritizing work
34.	Encouraging quality and excellence	70.	Remaining slightly detached
35.	Being 'one of the boys'	71.	Willing to consider innovation
36.	Grasping new opportunities	72.	Encouraging initiative

Figure 4.1 What makes a good manager?

Power torch

This is a short exercise published in 1999, specifically designed by the Small Firms Enterprise Development Initiative (SFEDI, 1999) for owner-managers, to encourage them to review their personal effectiveness in running their businesses. The first stage comprises fourteen questions which can help to identify potential areas for improvement within the business. The second part contains a series of more focused questions about cash flow management and the impact of your personal performance on the business. The questions are linked to the NVQ Level 4 Business Management and Development Standards, and the booklets are available from SFEDI. As with the previous exercise, the sample action plan (Figure 4.2) can be used for any areas of development that are identified as a result of this exercise.

Planning and prioritizing your work

Activity

Make a list of all of the daily activities that waste your valuable time, e.g. talking to the secretary, making coffee, smoking breaks, failing to delegate routine tasks, cluttered desk, allowing interruptions, lack of self-discipline, unfinished work brought forward, attending unnecessary meetings, responding to crises, long lunch breaks, playing golf during working hours etc.

Make a second list of ways in which you could save time, e.g. better use of diary to plan work, delegate more work, keep meetings to tighter agendas and timescales.

How do these compare? Highlight key areas for improvement, and work out how the improvements can be achieved, and how you will measure their achievement.

Activity

List all the items of work that you have to do over the next two weeks, under two headings. First, the proactive work that will lead to profit or development of the business (sales meetings with customers, planning new products or services, etc.). Second, list the reactive and routine work which has to be completed, but which does not really contribute to the profitability or growth of the business (VAT returns, reports for bank managers, filing and administration, etc.). Then prioritize your tasks under four headings:

1   *Important – urgent*: typically the proactive tasks that need a prompt response, such as customer enquiries, ensuring the completion of customer orders and the delivery of goods on time.

2   *Important – less urgent*: typically the proactive work that will lead to growth of the business in the longer term. This may involve negotiations for future contracts, development of new products and markets, negotiations with suppliers, etc.

3   *Less important but urgent*: the day-to-day work that needs prompt action, but which does not necessarily involve substantial time commitment, e.g. writing cheques and letters, paying bills, renewing insurance policies, advertising for staff.

4   *Less important and less-urgent*: the routine work which is not due for completion in the next week or two, e.g. the quarterly VAT returns, monthly PAYE records, non-urgent replies to letters, etc. But beware of this category because less important and less urgent work, if repeatedly deferred, has a habit of suddenly becoming both urgent and important, particularly if it involves late VAT returns!

How did you perform in these two activities? Are you already using your time effectively? Are you already planning and prioritizing your work, or was this a new experience for you? Have you identified any scope for further improvement? If so, what changes will you make, and how will you start to implement these?

Identifying personal goals and objectives

The previous exercises have been concerned with identifying the skills needed to ensure the efficient operation of the business, but it is equally important for the owner-manager not to neglect the personal aspirations and objectives of his or her family:

- Where am I now, and where do I want to be in five or ten years' time?

- What material benefits do I expect to gain from running my own business, in terms of my salary, my home, my car, holidays, etc.?

- What benefits do my family expect from the business?

- Are my family aware of the potentially substantial commitments of time and effort involved in establishing and running a business? Are they prepared to accept possible disruption to family routines, and possible financial pressures during the early stages of setting up the business?

- What price am I prepared to pay in terms of stress and risk to personal health, in order to ensure that the business succeeds?

- How will I measure the success of the business in material terms?

- How will I measure the success of the business in terms of my of job satisfaction and self-fulfilment?

- What will I do when I have achieved my targets?

- Will I be able to handle failure if the business does not work out?

- Are my family fully aware of the risks involved?

- Do I have the will to succeed?

These are just a selection of the questions which potential owner-managers should be considering not just on their own, but in consultation with their spouses, domestic partners or families. There may be times when an owner-manager needs the support of friends and families, and that support is likely to be more forthcoming if their own objectives and aspirations have been considered. Once again, where targets are identified, action plans can be prepared to monitor progress and achievement, and the review of those plans should be carried out not in isolation, but in conjunction with partners and family.

Apart from being yet another essential part of the required NVQ evidence, there is a very sound reason for the preparation of action plans because, with the best will in the world, personal objectives can easily slip or be pushed into the background. Think back to last year. How many New Year's resolutions did you actually manage to keep, or have you

Action plans for self-development

Skills/competencies to be improved	Activities/methods of improvement	Means of measuring achievement	Degree of success/ reasons for failure
Example :			
			Are there still jobs to be delegated?
Effective delegation – Work needs to be delegated to release time for other management duties.	Review daily/ weekly job activities to see which of these could be delegated. Select potential staff & assess their suitability to take responsibility, and any training needs etc. Define staff objectives and how their progress and achievement will be monitored and assessed against their targets. Review own workload once more.	Is delegated work progressing suitably well? If not, why not? Are there still more jobs that I can delegate? What else am I doing with my time? Review progress after 30 days, and 60 days.	What problems have occurred?

Figure 4.2   Action plan for self-development

simply given up trying? Owner-managers are very busy people, and in their case it is even more important to make some public or tangible declaration of intent, in the form of a self-development action plan, to ensure it will be not be forgotten or relegated into oblivion by the sheer pressures of work. A simple action plan, in the form of the example shown in Figure 4.2, pinned in a prominent (although not necessarily public) location, will act as a regular reminder.

Another reason for the use of an action plan is to provide a means of monitoring progress on a regular basis, and to set specific review dates. To take an analogy: how many times have you heard someone say 'I'm going on a diet and I intend to lose ten pounds'? Okay, when will you start, right now or after the barbecue next week? When will you lose the ten pounds, by next month, next year or by Christmas 2010? How often will you check your progress, daily, weekly, monthly, never? And if you do manage to hit your target weight, how will you ensure that it does not go up again?

The answer is easy: 'I will use my action plan to set specific targets and review dates to monitor my progress, and to highlight any problems or reasons for failure, along with the necessary corrective action.' Well, is that not exactly how the Weight Watchers organization helps its members to succeed, albeit in a slightly different format and with a bit of added guilt for motivation?

So, to review the process of action planning:

1   What skills gaps do I wish to fill? What competencies do I wish to improve? List them.

2   What methods or activities will I undertake in order to facilitate the development of those skills and competencies? Again, list them, and review them to ensure that they are appropriate.

3   How will I measure my progress or success? Set specific targets, set review dates and set target dates for achievement. Define the criteria for success.

4   How well has the process worked? What problems were encountered? What were the reasons for success or failure? Where do I go from here?

The self-assessment process is not a one-off activity that you go through when you set up a new business. It is a measure of an effective manager that personal skills and capabilities are reviewed on a regular basis. If you were employed by a large organization, you would almost certainly be involved in some form of annual or twice-yearly appraisal system. You may well have plans for setting up such a system in your own business. So why should you not bother to carry out regular assessment on yourself? Self-evaluation is not just a process of assessing skills gaps and development needs, it is also about your overall performance as a business manager:

Effective management requires regular self-evaluation

- *In the achievement of standards*: meeting objectives and deadlines, ensuring consistent quality of work, achieving targets, achieving and maintaining customer satisfaction.

- *In the efficient use of time*: prioritizing work, effective delegation and allocation of work, monitoring progress of work, and avoiding time-wasting activities.

- *As part of self-development*: improving and upgrading skills and abilities, improving personal knowledge. This is the process described as Continuous Professional Development (CPD).

- *In the style of management*: employing and varying management styles according to the needs of the situation (autocratic, democratic etc.); being proactive and in control, thinking ahead and anticipating problems, rather than being reactive and constantly fire-fighting in response to problems.

Reference

Palmer, G. (1999). *Personal Effectiveness.* (You and Your Business booklets) SFEDI.

Further reading

Palmer, S. (1998). *People and Self Management.* Butterworth-Heinemann.

Chapter 5 Identifying relevant legislation

Chapter 5
Chapter 5

The sheer volume of legislation, rules, statutes and directives facing small firms seems to have increased at an exponential rate, even more so as the UK is drawn ever closer into the tangled web of the European Union where bureaucracy rules supreme and the harmonization of the laws of its member states appears to be the sole acknowledged route to Nirvana. Why, I ask, should anyone want to go to heaven if they can get a job as a bureaucrat or, better still, a solicitor in Brussels? However, coming back to the real world, actually identifying the legislation which is relevant to any particular new small business can be a nightmare, even without the fact that the laws are constantly changing and thereby placing additional demands on owner-managers who have to understand and comply with them.

The objective of this chapter is to list and briefly describe a range of the most important pieces of legislation which might affect small businesses and their owners. The intention is not so much to produce a legal compendium or reference text, as to assist the readers to identify those areas of the law which are relevant to their own particular businesses, and where they will need to examine the implications of that legislation in more detail. Remember, ignorance is no excuse in the eyes of the law so, if a piece of legislation sounds remotely relevant to your business circumstances, check it out.

This chapter covers much of the underpinning knowledge requirements of Unit A3 of NVQ Level 3 Business Planning, entitled 'Investigate the requirements of any legislation you have to comply with in setting up and running the business'. Unit A3 relates to setting up and operating the business legally, and to identifying any health and safety and environmental legislation which might be appropriate to the particular business. For the NVQ candidate, it is as important to identify which legislation is not relevant to a particular business proposition, and to be able to explain why that is so; as it is to pick out those laws which are relevant. This is because the justified or argued elimination of legislation which is not relevant to the business, is a valuable means of demonstrating the candidate's competence, knowledge and understanding of the subject.

Many organizations will be subject to very specific legislation which is only relevant to their own particular field of operation (e.g. abattoirs, breweries, fishing, road transport or zoos), and it is simply not practical to try to address all of these. Instead, this chapter looks at the main items of legislation, which have applications to broad sections of business operations, and groups these under five headings:

- health and safety and related legislation;

- environmental and trading legislation;

- employment law;

- financial and company law;

- anti-discrimination law.

Health and safety legislation

Health and safety legislation has existed under a number of guises for many years, but it was only in the 1970s that its real importance was acknowledged and made properly enforceable. Prior to that the emphasis was made, for example, on provision of safety guards on machinery, but without enforcing their use, or for ensuring adequate toilet facilities where more than five staff were employed. Post-1974 the emphasis switched to that of care for employees, visitors, customers and passers-by, and to risk assessment and prevention of accidents in the work-place.

Factories Act 1961 and Offices, Shops and Railway Premises Act 1963

Under the Factories Act the employer ('occupier' of the factory) has a responsibility to protect the employees against any risks of the industrial environment to which they might be regu-larly exposed. This involves ensuring safe systems of work, safe access and clear gangways, and fenced and guarded machinery. Occupation of premises and the name and nature of the busi-ness must be notified to the Health and Safety Executive, including notification if any mechanical machinery is used. Written details of any death or serious injury resulting from industrial accidents must also be notified within three days of the incident. Under the Offices, Shops and Railway Premises Act prospective occupants must notify the appropriate local authority at least one month before the start of occupation of the premises; and must subsequently notify any accidents or industrial diseases. Safety requirements required by the Act are similar to those specified under the Factories Act, but employers must also avoid overcrowding premises, and must provide adequate water and sanitation facilities, heating, lighting, venti-lation and first-aid facilities.

Health and Safety at Work Act 1974

Whereas the previously mentioned Acts were fundamentally concerned with the provision of basic minimum standards of safety and hygiene in the workplace, the Health and Safety at

Work Act was designed to extend this provision (and the employers' liability to ensure it) much further. It is the duty of the employer to provide safe working systems and a safe and secure working environment for all staff, customers and visitors to premises, as well as the general public, passers-by and, in some cases, even potential trespassers. The Act applies not only to business premises, but to all public places, local authority premises, hospitals, entertainment sites, community halls, shopping centres, etc. Responsibility also extends to any staff working away from the main place of work, such as lorry drivers, or contractors' staff working on site. It also requires sites to be securely fenced against intruders who might inadvertently injure themselves on a hazard within the site. Long gone are the days when building site workers would lean over the side of scaffolding to wolf-whistle at passing girls. These days, apart from probably being accused of sexual harassment, the chances are that most scaffolding will be covered by a mesh screen to prevent any loose objects falling on passers-by, and leaning over the scaffolding would be regarded as an unsafe practice. If television adverts for a certain popular fizzy drink are anything to go by, it will probably be the girls doing the whistling anyway!

Another major requirement of the Act is the need for every employer with more than five staff to produce and regularly update a written Health and Safety Policy Document for the organization or premises, and to ensure that all new and existing staff are made aware of its contents. Employers are also required to carry out regular risk assessments throughout their premises, and across working practices, to identify and minimize any likely potential harm to employees or potential users or visitors to the premises. Appropriate health and safety posters must also be clearly displayed within the premises, and these can be obtained from the local Health and Safety Executive (HSE) offices. Employers must record all accidents or injuries in an accident book kept for that purpose. The HSE must be notified of any deaths or major injuries resulting from accidents at work, and can prosecute employers or owners or operators of premises for negligence if appropriate, the penalties for which are potentially high and in extreme cases might include imprisonment.

Control of Substances Hazardous to Health (COSHH)

All employers and operators of premises where potentially hazardous chemicals are stored, manufactured or used in a commercial or industrial process must carry out specific risk analyses under the COSHH regulations. As part of this process, they must identify suitable preventative actions or remedies in the event of accident, leakage or spillage of any such substances. They must also display appropriate warning notices detailing the nature and potential hazards of the substances, and have the means available to deal with any such events. Staff must be instructed in the safe handling and storage of hazardous substances, and informed of what to do if leakage or spillage should occur.

For example, most agrochemical distributors are required to have impervious flooring and some form of concrete bund around the site so that any leakage can be contained to avoid the contamination reaching local drains or watercourses. Within the site they would have to have sand or other inert substances to soak up spillage, and masks for staff to avoid breathing noxious fumes. Whilst this might sound like an extreme example, most industrial cleaning agents contain bleach or chemicals which might come under COSHH regulations, and even the peroxides and perm lotions used by hairdressers can have some quite damaging effects on human skin if mishandled!

Reporting of Injuries, Diseases and Dangerous Occurrences Regulations 1982

These regulations, often referred to as RIDDOR, require the owners or operators of businesses or premises to notify the responsible authorities of certain specific events or illnesses. For example, the local Environmental Health Authority would need to be notified of an outbreak of food poisoning, particularly if it involved the staff of a food manufacturer or distributor, or the customers of a specific catering outlet. The HSE must be notified of any major accidents or substantial injuries to employees, and the local Medical Officer must be notified of outbreaks and individuals who contract specified illnesses such as meningitis or polio.

Fire regulations

The local fire brigade is responsible for advising operators of premises and for inspecting the premises to ensure that they comply with fire regulations. These will vary according to the size, type and use of premises. For example, a small workshop may just require a specified number of water and powder fire extinguishers, whereas a restaurant kitchen will also usually need to have fire blankets available to cover any burning cooking oil. At a more complex level, a residential home or hotel will have to provide fire exits and escape routes, emergency lighting, regularly tested alarm systems, staff training, and fire-doors at regular intervals along corridors, which are designed to withstand fire for certain minimum periods. Unless the premises comply with the regulations, the fire brigade may refuse to issue or renew the necessary licence, and the hotel will be unable to operate. Fire regulations may also be relevant to materials used for partitioning within offices, to storage of inflammable materials and to the external access routes to premises.

These types of legislation have been linked together as being in the interests of members of the public at large, both in terms of protecting their interests as consumers and their interests in the protection of the living environment as a whole.

Environmental and trading legislation

Environmental Health Act

The Environmental Health Department of local authorities are particularly concerned with aspects of public hygiene and food safety. In the case of public health and hygiene, the Environmental Health Act empowers local authorities to carry out or enforce the safe removal and disposal of refuse, and the extermination of vermin or other risks to public health. They are also responsible for monitoring and licensing the operation of funeral parlours.

In recent years the food safety role has become much more prominent, with all manufactures, suppliers, distributors, and retailers of food or drink having to register with their local authority. Specific standards are prescribed for the safe preparation, handling and storage of food, and premises are regularly inspected to ensure that these standards are met on an ongoing basis. There is the risk of enforced closure of premises in cases of default, and heavy fines where food poisoning is found to result from poor food handling or contamination, which is quite realistic when we remember that the clostridium and streptococcal bacteria found in kitchens are potentially lethal.

The food-handling regulations prescribe minimum levels of training for staff, i.e. the Basic Food Hygiene Certificate, with higher levels for supervisors. They also prescribe the types of washable materials suitable for covering walls, ceilings and floors, fly screens for protecting windows and vents, the quality of stainless steel for work surfaces and the colour coding of knives etc. used for different purposes to avoid cross-contamination. Operators of food premises are expected to produce, adhere to and record regular planned cleaning programmes for all food production areas, to provide staff with all necessary protective clothing and to provide instruction and supervision in safe food-handling practice.

Town and Country Planning Acts 1971

The principle of development control was introduced in 1947 under the first Town and Country Planning Acts, which were updated in 1971. Local planning authorities such as the district councils are responsible for producing local development plans, controlling and approving new developments, approving the change of use of premises and monitoring the use of specific 'listed' buildings and conservation areas. County councils have a role in producing strategic plans and for development control of more major items such as mining, gravel extraction, waste disposal etc.

For any new or expanding business which is planning to occupy premises, it is necessary to ensure that planning approval exists to cover the type of activity for which the premises will be used. For example, if I wish to convert the front room of my home into a shop, I will need to obtain permission for change of use from domestic to retail use. If I wish to rent a farmer's barn to manufacture and sell rustic furniture, I will need to apply for change of use from agricultural to commercial use. Remember, simply applying for change of use for premises does not mean the new use can start straight away. The change of use still has to be approved, and very often there will be specific planning conditions attached to the approval. For example, approval may be granted for a fixed period such as three, five or ten years, it may prohibit any structural change to the premises without further specific approval or it may limit hours of opening or public access.

Building Regulations

Whereas the planning regulations affect the use that can be made of premises, the Building Regulations relate to any changes or modifications to the structure of the premises, including drainage. If I wish to build a conservatory on the back of my house, so long as it falls within a certain size limit, I will not need planning permission; but I will still need Building Regulations approval for the new structure. When an application is made, the plans are submitted to the local council and a building inspector or surveyor will check and approve the structural details, e.g. whether or not the foundations are adequate to support the proposed building. Once building commences, the inspector will visit the premises at specific intervals, to ensure that the builder is actually complying with the details of the plans, and the inspector has the power to stop work or order work to be replaced or improved if inadequate. Naturally, the local council charges a fee for the Building Regulations approvals and inspections.

Local Government Miscellaneous Provisions Act 1982

This is an interesting piece of legislation that gives local authorities discretionary powers to license and/or inspect various business activities. For example, in some districts, all beauticians and massage parlours need to register with the local council. In others, only those performing functions that penetrate the skin (such as tattooing, ear piercing or electrolysis) need to register and be inspected for hygiene purposes. So, in view of the discretionary nature of this Act, if in doubt, call your local council offices to check first.

Control of Pollution Act 1974

This Act was introduced both to update and reinforce some previous legislation, such as the Clean Air Act; and to cover emerging problems and gaps in environmental controls. These included the emission of gases and toxic fumes, pollution of watercourses, and the licensing and control of tipping and disposal of waste materials. For example, every tip site, waste storage or waste transfer station has to be licensed, usually by the county council or local authority with responsibility for waste disposal (as opposed to waste collection). The licence will specify the materials which can be processed or tipped at the site. If any toxic or problematic materials are to be handled, then the conditions of the licence will usually specify the measures that need to be taken for safety purposes. Certain toxic materials can only be disposed above impervious clay soils as a sandy or chalky substratum might allow them to permeate into an underground aquifer and pollute a water supply. I was once involved in a site in Sheffield where a limestone barrier was proposed to stop an underground fire in a very old coke-breeze tip from reaching a coal seam on adjacent land. These are problems inherited from an industrial past, which the Control of Pollution Act is intended to prevent from recurring in the future. It does have very significant implications for any manufacturers whose processes result in the need to store or dispose of toxic materials.

Sale of Goods Act 1979 and 1995, and Consumer Protection Act 1987

These pieces of legislation are designed to protect the interests of the consumer, and are primarily administered by the Trading Standards Officers employed by local authorities. They define the rules under which warranties can be enforced, goods exchanged, refunds obtained, etc. At one time the key definition was that when goods are sold, they must be 'fit for the purpose' for which they were designed or of 'merchantable' quality. The latter phrase has now been replaced by the term 'reasonable quality', which in many ways swings the balance more in favour of the consumer. In the first instance it is the vendor of the goods who is legally responsible to the consumer for any faults or problems, including those inherent in the product itself, but ultimately the cost of repair or replacement goes back to the manufacturer (or importer). In the case of death or substantial personal injury, the liability may extend to all parties with involvement in the product: manufacturer, importer, carrier, wholesaler and retailer. The law requires that terms of trade are expressed in plain and intelligible language. They must not contain any terms that bias the transaction unfairly or unreasonably against the consumer, and inclusion of such terms would render those contracts null and void. In particular they cannot seek to restrict liability or enforce broad indemnities for personal death or injury and any clauses seeking to restrict liability for loss or damage must be reasonable in the circumstances. For example, the manufacturer's warranty or guarantee cannot limit or restrict the consumer's rights as defined in law; neither can it attempt to limit the manufacturer's legal liability for negligence.

Where vendors and manufacturers fail to meet their responsibilities to the consumer, or where goods are considered to be dangerously faulty, then the Trading Standards Officers have powers of prosecution. These days it is quite common for most of the larger high street chain stores to offer refund and replacement facilities which go far beyond the minimum legal requirements, and this can reflect badly on the smaller independent traders who do not have the resources to provide the same terms.

Advertising standards

These are not so much statutory regulations, but a code of standards that are designed to encourage good practice within the advertising industry, and to discourage adverts which are considered in bad taste, offensive, inaccurate misleading or libellous. The code of practice is administered by the Advertising

Standards Authority, which itself was set up by the government for the purpose.

Data Protection Act 1984

Under this Act all computer users who store details or information about private individuals, or information of a personal nature, must register with the Data Protection Registrar. This ruling applies whether the holders of the information are private individuals, sole traders, partnerships, limited companies or public limited companies. It does not apply, however, to information about individuals which is stored on manual systems such as card index files. The onus is on the holder of computer data to register under the Act, and not to wait until registration is queried or challenged.

Anyone who thinks that their personal data might be stored within a computer system has a right to be informed if that is the case, and a right to see the stored information on payment of a reasonable fee. For example, the two biggest credit reference agencies which operate in the UK will provide a copy of any information held against a named individual or private address on payment of a fee, which is currently £2. This enables people who are refused credit to check on whether or not the reason for refusal might be based on erroneous or inaccurate information.

Employment law

Employment law is a very complicated and constantly changing subject. For that very reason, all businesses are well advised to seek professional guidance where disputes or areas of doubt might arise, as the consequential expenses and risks of facing industrial tribunals can be crippling to a small business which is struggling to establish itself. Even professional personnel managers who subscribe to receive regular updates to changes in the law still have to think carefully when giving advice. So, it is even more important for the owner-manager, who must double as the firm's personnel specialist, to tread carefully.

Employment Acts

Many of the provisions of the various Employment Acts overlap with other legislation, described below. Fundamentally, in law the employer is obliged to:

- provide a safe and secure working environment;

- pay staff at agreed rates and at agreed intervals;

- provide staff with contract of employment;

- inform staff of health and safety policies, and discipline and grievance procedures;

- ensure that staff do not exceed permitted working hours;

- provide staff with paid leave for holidays, statutory sickness pay, paid maternity leave;

- pay staff for redundancy as appropriate, and give suitable notice to terminate employment;

- treat staff fairly and reasonably, particularly where dismissal is concerned;

- not discriminate against staff in any way.

In return, the employer has the right to expect staff to:

- put in a fair day's work for a fair day's pay;

- observe workplace rules and health and safety policy;

- act in a safe, competent and reasonable way alongside other employees;

- act honestly, and not against the employers' interests;

- take care of the employer's property;

- honour the employer's ownership of any patents or inventions developed within work time or in the workplace;

- not disclose any confidential information about the business to outsiders;

- obey lawful and reasonable instructions from the employer.

Employment Protection Act 1975

This gives employees who have been with an organization for at least two years, automatic rights to, and guarantees of, the minimum levels of statutory redundancy pay if faced with that prospect. They are also allowed paid time off work to look for alternative work if facing redundancy. After six months of employment, female staff are entitled to receive statutory maternity pay and, after two years in employment, their jobs must be kept open for them if they wish to return to work after their period of maternity leave. Also after two years, employees have the right (with legal redress via industrial tribunal) not to be unfairly dismissed from employment. Since 1995, all of these rights apply to part-time as well as full-time workers.

European Working Hours Directive 1998

The UK, by opting out of the EU Social Chapter, had previously avoided having to implement the Working Hours Directive. However, as many EU countries felt that the opt-out gave the UK an unfair trading advantage, it was resurrected under the auspices of EU health and safety legislation. It came into force in the UK in October 1998 and basically requires that no employee shall work in excess of an average of forty-eight hours per week over any seventeen-week rolling period. Employers must take 'all reasonable steps' to ensure compliance with the Directive. As is immediately obvious, for any substantially sized organization running a shift system, the calculations and administration involved are horrendous and, whereas larger organizations should be more able to accommodate the cost incurred therein, for smaller firms that cost constitutes another substantial overhead burden.

Certain professions (such as doctors) are exempt from the Directive, and there is a clause that permits employees to opt voluntarily for exemption from the forty-eight hour limit. However, for that voluntary option to be valid, there must be no pressure from the employer and the employee's approval must be given in writing. For it to continue, employees must regularly (e.g. at six-month intervals) be given the option to change their minds or renew their decision to opt out of the Directive.

The Directive also specifies minimum breaks (eleven hours) between periods of work, plus a minimum break of twenty-four hours in each seven-day week and a compulsory rest break if working more than six hours in a day. The minimum paid annual leave entitlement of at least three weeks, was raised to a minimum of four weeks per year in 1999. Again, the resulting financial burden of funding extra paid holidays will have a substantial impact on the operating costs of many smaller businesses.

Contracts of Employment Act 1972

Within two months of starting employment, every employee must be provided with a written contract of employment which specifies the nature and location of their work, the rate and methods of payment, hours of work, holiday entitlement, period of notice, etc. If the employee has not already been informed of the organization's health and safety policy, this should normally be provided at the same time, along with a copy of any discipline and grievance procedures. Whilst these do not actually form part of the contract of employment, their provision both constitutes good practice and, in the case of the health and safety policy, forms part of the employers duty under that legislation.

Employer's Liability (Compulsory Insurance) Regulations 1972 and 1998

All organizations, whether they are sole traders, large commercial businesses, public sector bodies, educational institutions or charities, if they employ any staff in any capacity, part-time or full-time, must take out employer's liability insurance to cover their staff for the risk of accident or injury in the workplace. A copy of the current certificate of insurance must be displayed in a prominent position on their premises, where it can be seen by employees. From January 1999 the minimum sum to be insured increased from £2 million to £5 million for any one claim, and employers are now required to keep all past insurance certificates for a period of forty years.

Minimum wage regulations

In October 1998, under an EU Directive, the government introduced a basic minimum wage for all employees of £3.60 per hour with a slightly lower level for very young employees. Whilst seen by many people as a positive social move, the wisdom of this is still arguable, as some employers have simply removed other staff benefits (such as paid tea breaks) to offset the cost. In some cases, others who may previously have paid higher rates now regard this as the industry accepted standard, and have reduced wages accordingly. Certainly for some poorly paid staff such as carers, domestic and security staff, the minimum wage is a positive move, but for many newly established or struggling small firms it simply increases overhead costs. Either way, it is a legal requirement with which businesses must now comply.

These are grouped together primarily because the laws which relate to the legal format and structure of businesses invariably, within the definition of those, become involved with the financial aspects of capitalization and distribution of profits, which in turn have implications for taxation etc.

Financial and company law

Finance Acts

The Finance Acts are the means by which the government is able to raise money by taxation, and to operate its fiscal policy. As such, they are effectively revised or modified every time there is a new government budget, which is usually at least once a year. However, they also define some of the processes and procedures within which businesses must operate, and act as a convenient mechanism to modify other more significant pieces of legislation. An example of the latter is shown below under the Partnership Act section.

HM Customs and Excise VAT regulations

Value added tax is another legacy of membership of the EU, the rates of which have climbed slowly but steadily since its introduction, to the current level of 17.5 per cent. The tax is based on the concept that at each stage of the supply or production of goods or services, value is added to those goods or services, and that added value is taxed. Some products, such as food, childrens' clothing, animal feeds, etc. are zero rated and attract no VAT. Currently, any business which has a sales turnover of £50 000 or more per annum, must register with

HM Customs and Excise and must charge VAT on the value of its invoices to customers. It must pay to Customs and Excise, every quarter, the sum of all VAT collected in that quarter, less any VAT which it has paid to its suppliers during the same period. Dates for payment are fixed and penalties for transgression can be heavy. Be warned! Unlike other creditors, Customs and Excise do not need to obtain a court order before sending the bailiffs into your premises to confiscate your stock or equipment.

Laws of taxation

These are essentially derived from the Finance Acts as principles in law, but the specific operation of the tax system (in terms of rates of taxation, tax-free allowances etc.) are modified each year by the government as part of the annual Budget. Amendments to taxes, and the introduction of new taxes are usually made under changes to tax regulations, rather than by introducing specific new Acts of Parliament. The influence of the EU on tax law is expected to become increasingly significant over the next few years, because of the pressure from several continental companies for the UK to 'harmonize' its tax laws with those of other parts of Europe. This is largely because some of our European neighbours regard the UK's less onerous company tax system as giving UK businesses an unfair advantage! Whatever happened to the old adage 'If you can't stand the heat, get out of the kitchen'? The laws on taxation are quite complicated, and this is one particular area where the advice of an accountant or taxation specialist can often more than pay for what it costs. Remember, tax avoidance is legal, tax evasion is not. The two are often finely divided, with the difference between them being only accurately determinable by an experienced taxation expert.

Companies Act 1985 and 1989

The Companies Act formulates the rules under which all limited companies, and public limited companies operate. It specifies the registration requirements, and the annual returns which have to be made, reporting the accounts and financial situation of the company etc., including:

- The annual accounts: profit and loss account, balance sheet, cash flow statement, debtors and creditors figures, details of any material changes in methods of accounting.

- The capital value of the company, numbers and types of shares issued, paid-up share value, details of loans and debentures, and any investments made by the company.

- The proposed dividend payable to shareholders.

- The names of directors, details of directors' expenses, remuneration of lowest and highest paid directors, schedule of directors' interests, directors' annual report.

- The names of auditors, details of auditor's remuneration, auditor's annual report.

For small companies with a turnover of under £350 000, and balance sheet of under £1.4 million, non-audited accounts with an abbreviated balance sheet can be submitted if supported by an accountant's statement confirming that the accounts agree with company records. A copy of the directors' report and the profit and loss account must be provided to shareholders.

In either case, the company must hold an annual general meeting to which all shareholders are invited. Day-to-day management is carried out by the board of directors.

Partnership Act 1890

As can be seen by the date, this is a very long-standing statute. When a partnership is established it is usual for the partners (or their legal representatives) to produce a legally binding partnership agreement which specifies a number of details:

- The names and addresses of the partners.

- The name and the nature of the business, and its trading activities.

- The effective date of commencement of the partnership.

- Decision-making procedures, and any arbitration or dissolution arrangements.

- The relative capital inputs of the partners.

- Banking arrangements, accounting periods, production of annual accounts etc.

- The way in which profits and losses will be divided and, if necessary, arrangements made with creditors.

The partnership agreement, once signed and witnessed, is a legally binding document. In the absence of a formal partnership agreement, the Partnership Act specifies that profits and losses will be allocated equally between partners in the business. It also prescribes that if a partner wishes to resign, the whole partnership must be wound up and a new partnership formed by any remaining partners. This is obviously an onerous process, particularly in professional partnerships (accountants, solicitors etc.) where changes are relatively frequent. To overcome that problem Section 113 of the Finance Act 1988 allows for the production of a 'Notice of Election to Continue Partnership' wherein a partner could leave, or another join, without having to dissolve or rewrite the partnership agreement, thereby simplifying the whole system for income tax purposes.

Another key aspect of the Partnership Act is that it specifies the 'joint and several liability' of all partners for partnership debts, whereby each partner is liable not only for their own share of the debt, but also for the debt as a whole, in the event of default by other partners.

Business Names Act 1985

Names of limited companies are registered with the Registrar of Companies at Companies House, and before a name is registered there is a search process to ensure that the name has not already been used by an allocated company or allocated to a newly formed but inactive company. The Registrar can provide advice on names, which must not be offensive or constitute a criminal offence.

In the case of partnerships or sole traders there is no registration requirement by law, and proprietors can use their own names or can trade under other names, e.g. 'John Smith trading as Wonder Web Internet Services'. It is a legal requirement however, for company letterheads and documents to show the registered company name and number, and the names of company directors, and the registered office. In the case of partners and sole traders, where they are not trading under their own names, they must be identified as proprietors on all business documents.

Copyrights, Designs and Patents Act 1988

As stated earlier, any inventions, designs or intellectual material produced by employees during working hours belong to the employer organization. Patent registration is a means of formally and legally establishing sole rights to an invention, and any competitors who wish to produce the same products will have to do so under licence from the patent holder.

However, patents are usually only granted for a fixed period of time, and once this expires the invention can be produced by anyone.

Copyright law usually relates to printed material, designs, drawings and graphics, electronic data, films and music. It does not protect the idea but prevents the copying of material by giving the owners of the copyright the legal right to sue anyone who breaches the copyright. In Britain, that protection lasts for seventy years. The copyright will usually belong to the author or creator of the material, although where this is an employee of a business, the copyright would normally belong to that business, it having commissioned the work.

Consumer Credit Act 1974

There are two aspects of this legislation of relevance to small firms. The first is that any business advising about or giving or arranging extended credit for customers, such as hire purchase or leasing agreements, must be licensed to operate under this Act. The other aspect is that of unincorporated businesses (sole traders and partnerships) where any loans raised by individual proprietors for business purposes, and which are less than £15 000, are regulated under the terms of this Act. These terms include appropriate 'cooling off' periods after signing, during which the borrower can change their mind; and the requirement that once a fixed proportion of repayments have been made, recovery of goods or enforcement of payment requires a court order.

Insolvency Act 1986 and Company Directors Disqualification Act 1986

One of the main objectives of the Insolvency Act Act was to curtail the legal but improper practice of operating what were known as 'phoenix' companies, particularly in the building and double glazing industries. This is the practice trading for a while, accruing debts, bleeding the business of cash by paying high directors' salaries and then liquidating businesses overnight. A new limited company surfaces a few days later under another name, with the same directors, operating from the same premises, producing the same goods or services, but having dumped previous creditors without much hope of payment. The Insolvency Act made it a criminal offence for any individual or company director to knowingly continue to trade whilst insolvent. The penalty for failing to take corrective action, or for failing to inform creditors of an insolvent situation, involves the company directors being made personally liable for all company debts, being barred from future directorships and, in some cases, for facing charges of fraud.

It is also no longer possible for company directors to put businesses into voluntarily liquidation and appoint themselves as liquidators. One spin-off from this has been the upsurge in private insolvency practitioners (often described as vultures with accounting qualifications) and their agents, for whom this was almost a licence to print money, particularly during the early 1990s when the rate of bankruptcy amongst small firms hit an all-time high. Insolvency practitioners operate almost in a monopoly market, charging fees well above those of their fellow accountants, so that by the time the assets of the insolvent business are liquidated, and the fees paid, there is often nothing left for the remaining creditors. But on a positive note, it does mean that all bankruptcies and insolvencies are investigated and the reasons subsequently reported to the Department of Trade and Industry. It also facilitates a monitoring system so that company directors who are involved repeatedly in liquidated companies can be identified and, if necessary, barred from holding directorships or positions of authority in future for up to fifteen years.

Businesses which are profitable, but insolvent due to cash flow problems, can continue to trade by virtue of voluntary agreements with creditors wherein, if at least 60 per cent of creditors agree to forestall action to recover debts, the insolvent business can negotiate a planned schedule of repayments to creditors. If the required proportion of creditors agrees, then the voluntary agreement is legally binding on all creditors, as is the schedule of repayments. The Act also introduced the statutory demand for payment, whereby creditors could demand payment within twenty-one days, and if this was not made, they could apply for an immediate winding-up order against the business.

Contract law (debt recovery etc.)

This law is essentially different from any statutory law in that the laws of tort or contract have not been established and precisely defined by Act of Parliament, but have evolved over a period of time as a result of numerous cases in civil law which have formed established precedents. However, as a result of this process there are established procedures within the civil courts, which facilitate the recovery of debts that are proven under civil law, e.g. where failure to pay within a specific time has resulted in a breach of contract. These recovery processes are discussed in more detail in Chapter 8.

Property law

Like the civil law relating to tort or contracts, the law that affects purchase, ownership and leasing of property is a mixture of statutes and case law. Some aspects of these will be examined in more detail in Chapter 13. If anything, this is an area where proper legal advice is more important than just about any other, particularly where legal liabilities are concerned. One example which has always been contentious is that of long-term leases, where a leaseholder who sells on the remaining lease to another party will still remain liable for any subsequent debts on that lease (such as non-payment of ground rent by the new leaseholder). Similarly, if the new leaseholder becomes insolvent, the responsibility for the lease will revert to the original leaseholder.

Broadly speaking, you are not allowed to discriminate against any employees or applicants for vacant jobs, on the grounds of race, colour, religion, ethnic origin, gender or marital status.

Anti-discrim-ination law

Race Relations Act (1976) and the Equal Opportunities Commission

This was one of the earlier moves to prevent discrimination in the workplace, wherein it became illegal to discriminate against individuals on the basis of skin colour, race or ethnic origin or nationality. When recruiting, you must not discriminate when advertising the job or in determining the terms of the job offered. An employer must not knowingly allow discrimination to continue in the workplace, or to discriminate against staff when considering training or promotion opportunities, or when involved in selecting staff for redundancy or dismissal. A Code of Practice has been produced by the Commission for Racial Equality to guide and assist employers.

The Equal Opportunities Commission (EOC) takes a more positive approach to the problem of discrimination. It expounds that not only should we be discouraging discrimination on the basis of race, religion, colour, ethnic origin, gender, age, size, and disability, but that employers and communities should take a more positive role in giving people the opportunity for employment, promotion and training. The key to this is to judge people on their abilities and potential, rather than on their disability or ethnic origin. The EOC also produces a Code of Practice for the guidance of employers.

Disabled Persons Employment Act 1944

As a result of the many injured and disabled service personnel returning from military service, this Act was introduced to facilitate and improve employment opportunities for them. Any organization which employs more than twenty staff has a legal duty to ensure that at least 3 per cent of its employees are drawn from those registered as disabled; and that facilities are available in the workplace to accommodate them. This may sound quite onerous for employers, but it must be considered within the context of the Department for Education and Employment (DfEE) definition of disabled persons as those who are registered as disabled for employment purposes (i.e. holders of DfEE Green Cards). This does not mean that all such people are wheelchair bound or physically incapacitated, as many holders of Green Cards are simply restricted in the range of work which they can do. For example, someone with a back or leg injury may not be able to move heavy loads in a factory, but could be fully competent in a sedentary or clerical position in an office, where their disability would probably not even be noticed by their colleagues. However, they still contribute towards the 3 per cent quota of disabled staff.

Disability Discrimination Act 1995

Following on from the previously mentioned legislation, the Disability Discrimination Act is really an attempt to promote the inclusion of disabled persons in the workplace and, again, we are not just talking about severe disabilities, but anyone who qualifies for a DfEE Green Card. There has always been a tendency in the past, and not necessarily a conscious tendency, for anyone who admits on a application form to being registered as disabled to be overlooked during the recruitment process – even if the disability is only relatively minor. As in the example quoted above, a person with arthritis may be 'disabled' in terms of having limited leg movement or lifting capability, but could have excellent analytical, financial or computing skills which can be exercised whilst sitting down.

Under this Act, disabled individuals have the right not to be discriminated against either during the process of recruitment or within their employment. This also means that they must be given equal opportunity to receive training or to be considered for promotion. Employers must also provide reasonable means of physical access and working systems to allow them to exercise their rights.

Sex Discrimination Act 1975 and 1989

When advertising job vacancies, or when interviewing staff, it is unlawful to discriminate on the basis of gender. Certain exemptions do exist, for example, where gender is specifically relevant as a genuine qualification for the job, such as mineworkers where the working conditions are deemed unsuitable for women or rape counsellors where a male counsellor would be entirely inappropriate or unacceptable for the needs of the clients. No longer can a pub landlord advertise for a barmaid; the advert must be for a bar person. There are, of course, still those inventive characters who try to find a way around the system: 'Bar person wanted – must be capable of filling a size 14 red rubber gym-slip.' The mind boggles! This still constitutes sexual discrimination, as it gives preference to one gender over the other.

Equal Pay Act 1970

The Equal Pay Act stipulates that an employer must give men and women equal rates of pay and other employee benefits and pensions, terms of contract etc. where they are carrying out the same or similar jobs as each other. However, in some circumstances differences in pay and conditions are acceptable, for example, in jobs where specialist skills or knowledge are required differential rates can be paid to reflect differing levels of qualifications and/or experience, or perhaps extra annual leave may be allocated as a reward for long service.

Trade Union Reform and Employment Rights Act 1993

It is illegal to discriminate against members of staff on the grounds of trade union membership or participating in trade union activities (unless this interferes with normal working duties and has been carried out without the approval of management). You do not currently have to recognize trade unions, although this situation may change if the EU has its way; but you cannot prohibit staff from belonging to a trade union. Even if there is no trade union involved, staff consultation is still required where redundancy is a possibility or where the potential sale of the business would affect the livelihoods of more than twenty staff. You are entitled to receive at least seven days' notice of any official industrial action by trade union members, during which time members must be balloted. Failure to do so could render the trade union liable for any losses resulting from a breach of contracts with your commercial customers. Unofficial activity is not the responsibility of trade unions, but would no doubt constitute a breach of contract of employment by the participants, possibly justifying termination of employment.

Sources of information

The main purpose of this chapter has been to summarize the purpose and significance of the various key items of legislation which are relevant to a small business, and which corresponds to the NVQ Unit A3 'Investigate the requirements of any legislation you have to comply with in setting up and running the business'. However, there is one aspect which needs further mention, and that is the way in which information is sought and gathered. Element 3.4 of the NVQ involves the ways in which information is assessed and utilized. Essentially this involves ensuring that:

- When consulting or using any published sources of information you must check to make sure that they are not out of date, and that the usefulness of the information has not been superseded by changes in circumstances or more recent events. For example, government population census information may be well prepared and reliable but, if it is only updated once every ten years, the 1991 census data will not be of much use in the year 2000. In contrast, internet data is often relatively new and regularly updated.

- The source of the data needs to be checked for its reliability. Again, although very dated, the population census data is generally accepted as coming from a reliable source, whilst the provenance of Internet data, although more current, may be less reliable. Data and statistics can easily be manipulated or modified to prove or disprove a particular argument, so the source and objectivity should be checked and carefully evaluated, especially if it is to be used as the basis for market research. Is the source reliable? Has the data been verified or evaluated by any external agency or academic institution?

- If you are unable to find the necessary information, or you need help in utilizing it, then you should turn to an appropriate person to get the right advice. For example, in the case of financial information, you might turn to an accountant, a bank manager or a business counsellor from the local enterprise agency. For advice on insurance, an independent insurance broker might be appropriate. In each case, it is important to ensure that the chosen adviser is suitably qualified and experienced for the job. There are many people who advertise themselves as offering accounting services, but a properly qualified accountant will display their qualifications, such as FCA, ACCA or CIMA. Similarly, you will find many local advertisements by financial advisers who might be able to give advice on personal investments and sell you an insurance policy or a private pension (and make plenty of commission for themselves in the process), but who are not qualified to give advice on business finance.

- As a rule of thumb, if you are in doubt about who to turn to for proper advice, try your local Citizens Advice Bureau or enterprise agency, who will generally be able to provide a list of names of suitable local people. Failing that, the local library will be able to give you the address of the relevant professional organization that can put you in touch with a local member. Finally, bear in mind before committing yourself to using a professional adviser, that these people have to make their living from the provision of advice and professional services, so be prepared to pay the going rate for their professional fees. If the thought of this bothers you, do not be afraid to ask them what the advice will cost before you commit yourself.

Further reading

Clayton, P. (1991). *Law for the Small Business*. Kogan Page.

Commission for Racial Equality (1976). *Code of Practice for the Elimination of Racial Discrimination and the Promotion of Equal Opportunity in Employment*. CRE.

Croner's Reference Book for Employers (updated bi-monthly). Croner Publications.

DTI (1996). *Setting Up in Business: A Guide to Regulatory Requirements*. DTI. URN 96/916.

DTI (1997). *Setting Up in Business: A Guide to Legislation Requirements*. DTI. URN 97/524.

Equal Opportunities Commission: Code of Practice. EOC.

Equal Opportunities Commission (1985). *Equal Opportunities: A Guide for Employers*. EOC.

Holmes, A. (1995). *Law for Small Businesses*. Pitman.

Keenan, A. (1993). *Company Law for Students*. Pitman.

Ruff (ed.) (1995). *Principle of Law for Managers*. Routledge.

Weaver, M. and Palmer, S. (1999). *Information Management*. Butterworth-Heinemann.

Chapter 6 Financial
Chapter 6 planning
Chapter 6

Financial planning is a fairly general term which covers a range of different activities, from the initial estimating of resource requirements and associated costs, forecasting sales revenue, identifying ongoing operating costs and preparing the budgetary plans which combine the former information. It also involves cash flow forecasting to ensure that there are no gaps between income and expenditure, analysing breakeven levels and forecasting profits.

It is because the process draws together all of the other aspects of planning the business, and then expressing those plans in monetary form, that it is so important to prepare correctly, as it is the primary point of interest for bankers and any other potential financiers or investors.

The objective of this chapter is to describe the various processes involved, and the reasoning behind them, so that the reader is in a position to prepare the necessary information for his or her own business plan. The sort of information which is required by bankers is also virtually identical to the evidence requirements of Unit A4 of the NVQ in Business Planning. In particular we shall be examining the financial forecasts specified in the evidence requirements for Element A4.3, cash flow, breakeven etc., individually and in more detail later in the chapter. As part of the process we shall also be defining and explaining some of the financial terminology which it is essential for the owner-manager to understand.

There are five key documents with which we are concerned, all of which are interlinked as they are developed from the same or overlapping information and the first two feed into the others:

- the owner-manager's own survival budget;
- the breakeven analysis;
- the budgetary plan;
- the cash flow forecast;
- the profit or loss forecast.

The personal survival budget

It may seem strange to start with this item, particularly as it is not really part of the information central to the business plan, but it does form an essential part of the budgetary plan and the cash flow forecast. The key question here is: 'If I am going into business for myself, how much money do I realistically need to draw from the business to maintain a reasonable and comfortable lifestyle?' Note carefully the wording here, in that we are not talking about a luxurious lifestyle (that hopefully comes later) and neither are we looking to find the minimum figure that we can survive on. If you are working hard, with long hours, substantial stress and risking your own personal resources, it is not unrealistic to expect to be able to draw sufficient income to enable you to live in basic comfort, especially if you have a family to support. You my find it quite acceptable to live on a very minimal budget during the early stages of the business, but there has got to be a cut-off point beyond which you must expect some comfort. If you fail to realize that fact yourself, then there will certainly come a point when your family will soon start to remind you of it, and probably in quite a firm manner, as financial pressures can strain any relationship, no matter how sound the latter may be. It really boils down to the fact that if you cannot achieve a basic reasonable lifestyle from your business, then you must ask yourself if the business is right for you in the first place.

The personal survival budget is effectively a summary of all your domestic outgoings over a period, typically a year, although for the purposes of your business budget you will no doubt break it down on a monthly basis. For example, for a family of two adults and two teenagers:

	£
Annual mortgage payments	3 600
Rates, water, sewage	900
Gas, electricity, telephone	900
Repairs and maintenance to home	300
Food and clothing for family	4 800
Loans, hire purchase, credit cards	600
Insurance policies, pension, savings	1 200
Car loan and running costs	3 600
Leisure, birthdays, Christmas, holidays	1 560
School travel, children's expenses.	780
Total:	18 240

Remember here, that the sum of £18 240 per annum (£1520 per month) does not constitute gross earnings, as it is the *minimum* sum which needs to be drawn from the business to pay for what is a far from exorbitant range of family expenses. As such it does not include any income tax or national insurance which must be paid on the gross figure. If the business is a limited company then, depending on tax allowances, the owner-manager would probably need to be paid a salary of at least £24,000 per annum to achieve the required net figure. In the case of a sole trader or partnership, the expected profit generated by the business would have to be sufficient to provide an after tax profit of around £19,000 to allow for drawings and Class 2 NIC. Otherwise owners would be eating into their own capital and almost certainly creating future cash flow problems and a shortage of working capital.

The break-even analysis

First we must define what we mean by 'breakeven', and in order to do this, we must distinguish between fixed costs and variable costs. Fixed costs are generally regarded as overhead costs, but the definition is that they remain 'fixed' in relation to changes in the level of sales or output. Typically they would include things like rent, rates, management and administration costs (including the owner-manager's own drawings), insurance etc. In contrast, variable costs are defined as those costs which vary directly in relation to changes in sales or output. This would include the costs of raw materials, components, labour production costs (particularly bonus pay or overtime), invoicing, packaging and distribution, etc. The breakeven point then is the point at which the revenue from sales equates to the variable costs incurred in achieving that level of sales, plus the full overhead cost. Put another way:

Sales revenue = fixed costs + variable costs + profit

When we are breaking even, by definition we are making no profit, so our sales revenue must be matching our fixed or overhead costs, plus what it cost us to make the goods we have already sold.

Another useful concept here is that of contribution, which can be found by turning around the above equation:

$$\text{Contribution (to profit and overheads)} = \text{selling price} - \text{variable cost}$$

Here we mean that the difference between the selling price and the variable cost of that item makes a contribution towards the profit and overheads of the business. For example, if a second-hand car dealer buys a car for £1000 (variable cost) and sells it for £1500 (selling price) then the difference of £500 makes a contribution to the dealer's overhead costs and profits.

There are several ways of calculating the breakeven point, including a graphical breakeven chart, but the two most accurate methods involve fairly simple calculations based on the above two equations. To illustrate this we will use the following example where selling price = £10 per unit, variable cost = £4 per unit, fixed costs = £150 000 per annum, and the breakeven sales level = Y units.

The equation method uses the simple formula mentioned above:

Sales = variable costs + fixed costs + profit

$10Y = 4Y + 150\,000 + 0$

$10Y - 4Y = 150\,000$

$6Y = 150\,000$

$Y = 150\,000 \div 6$

$Y = 25\,000$ units

So we see that when sales levels reach 25 000 units, the income is sufficient to cover the variable costs incurred, plus the total overhead costs. However, it is only when sales start to exceed this level that the revenue will make a contribution towards the profit of the business.

The contribution margin method uses a different equation:

$$\text{Breakeven level} = \frac{\text{fixed costs} + \text{net profit}}{\text{contribution}}$$

$$Y = \frac{150\,000 + 0}{10 - 4}$$

$$Y = \frac{150\,000}{6}$$

$$Y = 25\,000$$

When calculating profit margins and setting prices it is important to remember the effect that small changes can have on breakeven level. Using the above example, lets say that our marketing specialists had advised that a small change in the selling price, (£9 instead of £10) would generate an increase of 10 per cent in sales. It sounds good, but is it worthwhile? Using the equation method, $9Y = 4Y + 150\,000$, we find that the breakeven point Y is 30 000 units. Unfortunately for us, the increase of 10 per cent in sales volume has only shifted a total of 27 500 units, so we are worse off than before, as we actually needed a 20 per cent increase in sales to break even at £9 per unit.

The budgetary plan

A budget is a financial plan for an organization, detailing income and expenditure over a fixed period of time, typically an accounting period. So, the primary purpose of setting a budget is to enable us to forecast levels of income and expenditure over the coming year to tell us where our money is coming from and where it is going.

There are basically two ways of preparing a budget, the most popular of which is historically based, where we take the budget for the previous period and adjust it for known or anticipated changes. This is quite a simple and reliable process, assuming of course that the figures from the previous year have been prepared carefully and have turned out to be realistic. The problem with this process is, that any contingencies or slack previously built into the system are usually compounded by the effects of inflation, leading to ever increasing inaccuracies.

The second way is zero-based budgeting where the budget is formulated from scratch, ignoring the figures from previous years, and thereby forcing every single budget heading to be carefully analysed and individually justified. This process has tended to be unpopular, partly because it is time-consuming if done properly and partly because it is prone to error if short-cuts and guesswork are permitted in order to save time, and very often the justification of parts of the budget are historically based anyway.

Historical budgets can be too 'loose' leading to inefficiency, whilst zero-based budgets can be too 'tight' leading to inflexibility, but apart from the first year when all budgets are by definition zero based, the historical approach is by far the most popular and practical.

So, why do we bother with budgets? The answer is that they are a very useful and practical management tool, and act as a yardstick against which we can monitor:

- levels and fluctuations in sales revenue;
- sales trends and changes in demand;
- profitability and cash flow;
- changing costs of overheads, raw materials, labour, sales and marketing, transport and distribution, administration, etc.;
- the impact of advertising programmes on sales;
- working capital requirements;
- the effects of changes in interest rates and exchange rates on operating costs.

So, if it can do all of this for us, how do we go about it? The budget calculations are produced on a spreadsheet which is basically a grid containing row and column calculations. If the rows and columns have been prepared correctly, then all the totals across, and all of the totals down, should correspond when carried to the bottom right-hand corner. However, Murphy's First Universal Law of Cock-Ups is always there to ensure that it never works first time. There will always be one frustrating little error or typing mistake that invariably takes ages to find, and I defy any honest person to say that it has never happened to them. An example of a budget spreadsheet is shown in Figure 6.1. Note that all budget figures always exclude VAT charged and payable.

The first stage is to identify the key areas of income, distinguishing between income generated by sales of goods or services, and non-trading income, e.g. rent from subletting space. You may wish to subdivide the sales income to show revenue from different product groups, from different types of customer or carrying different profit margins. For example, a beer and wine wholesaler would want to distinguish between those two major product areas, but the budget headings may also differentiate between sales to retail outlets where a 20 per cent profit margin is expected, and sales to other wholesalers at a 10 per cent profit margin. The revenue figures throughout the year will also need to reflect seasonal trends. In the case of the wholesaler, this would involve peaks over the summer months and at Christmas, and much quieter periods during February to March and October to November. Any other sources of income are identified and included under a separate heading, e.g. capital receipts of loans, and then all items of income are totalled.

The next stage is to carry out a similar exercise for all known areas of expenditure, including overheads, operating costs, stock purchases (which should reflect sales levels) distributions costs, capital expenditure and loan repayments, etc. As with income, these are totalled for each month and for the year as a whole.

Item	Jan.	Feb.	March	April	May	June	July	August	Sept.	Oct.	Nov.	Dec.	Totals
INCOME:													
Market stall	£9,000	£12,000	£7,000	£9,000	£8,000	£10,000	£9,000	£8,000	£10,000	£11,000	£15,000	£17,000	£125,000
Non-trading income	£50	£50	£50	£50	£50	£50	£50	£50	£50	£50	£50	£50	£600
Total Income	£9,050	£12,050	£7,050	£9,050	£8,050	£10,050	£9,050	£8,050	£10,050	£11,050	£15,050	£17,050	£125,600
EXPENDITURE:													
Stall rent	£750	£600	£600	£750	£600	£600	£750	£600	£600	£750	£600	£600	£7,800
Stall wages	£500	£500	£400	£500	£400	£400	£500	£400	£400	£500	£400	£600	£5,500
Stall stock	£5,400	£7,200	£4,200	£5,400	£4,800	£6,000	£5,400	£4,800	£6,000	£6,600	£9,000	£10,200	£75,000
Bags and wrappings	£90	£120	£70	£90	£80	£100	£90	£80	£100	£110	£150	£170	£1,250
Stall fittings	–	–	£50	–	–	–	–	–	£50	–	–	£100	£100
Book-keeper	£30	£30	£30	£30	£30	£30	£30	£30	£30	£30	£30	£30	£360
Admin and expenses	£100	£80	£80	£100	£80	£80	£100	£80	£80	£100	£80	£80	£1,040
Advertising	£30	£60	£30	£30	£30	£30	£30	£30	£30	£30	£30	£60	£420
Insurance	£50	£50	£50	£50	£50	£50	£50	£50	£50	£50	£50	£50	£600
Transport – running costs	£250	£250	£250	£250	£250	£250	£250	£250	£250	£250	£250	£250	£3,000
Transport – hire purchase	£150	£150	£150	£150	£150	£150	£150	£150	£150	£150	£150	£150	£1,800
Bank loan repayments	£100	£100	£100	£100	£100	£100	£100	£100	£100	£100	£100	£100	£1,200
Bank charges	–	–	£300	–	–	£250	–	–	£250	–	–	£250	£1,050
Personal drawings	£1,500	£1,200	£1,200	£1,500	£1,200	£1,200	£1,500	£1,200	£1,200	£1,500	£1,200	£1,200	£15,600
Total Expenditure:	£8,950	£10,340	£7,510	£8,950	£7,770	£9,240	£8,950	£7,770	£9,290	£10,170	£12,040	£13,740	£114,720
NET INCOME	£100	£1,710	£-460	£100	£280	£810	£100	£280	£760	£880	£3,010	£3,310	£10,880

Figure 6.1 Winston Wight: 12-month budgetary plan

Case Study

Winston Wight

If you have ever driven down Lewisham High Street in South East London, you may have noticed that the two predominant products on sale are greengrocery and ladies' underwear. Winston Wight is a bright lad who owns one of these ladies' underwear stalls. He has just completed his second year of trading, and has produced a budget for his bank manager, with whom he has a small bank loan. His income comes primarily from sales of stock, with peaks in the pre-Christmas period and just before Valentine's Day. On Mondays when he is not working, he sublets his market stall, for £50 per month (non-trading income). He works on an average gross profit margin of 40 per cent, and apart from the rent on his stall, and the cost of running his van, his overheads are minimal. He pays no electricity, rates, water or sewage etc. He pays a book-keeper to maintain his accounts, and draws a regular sum of £300 per week from the business for his own living expenses. He also pays a wage to his girlfriend Sharon, who works with him part-time on the stall. His budget, shown in Figure 6.1, is a fairly simple and straightforward example of a spreadsheet. All relevant areas of expenditure are clearly identified, including adjustments for five-week months, and of course the figure in the bottom right-hand corner adds up correctly. We will come back to our friend Winston in the next section.

The third stage is to calculate the net income or expenditure for each month and for the year as a whole. If done correctly, this can be quite a complicated and time-consuming exercise the first time around. It is particularly important then, that the time invested is not wasted once the bank manager has seen it, by simply filing the budget in the cabinet and forgetting it until next year. The budget is a working document, but it will only work for you if you use it properly. The monthly figures against each item of income and expenditure are your forecasts, and the benefit of budgeting is only gained by the regular monthly monitoring of actual income and expenditure against those forecasts. By comparing the two, you will be able to identify discrepancies, and in searching for explanations to these you will further identify potential problem areas. Ignore the process, and you may find that the problems continue to grow unnoticed, until it may be too late to rectify them.

In many respects the preparation of a cash flow forecast resembles the process of preparing a budget spreadsheet, as the format and calculations are basically the same. However, the purpose of cash flow forecasts is different in that where the budget is concerned with identifying levels of income and expenditure for each part (e.g. month) of the budgetary period, the cash flow forecast is concerned with when that income is received and when payments are made for expenditure incurred. In order to do this the cash flow forecast will need to reflect:

The cash flow forecast

- cash-balances brought forward from the previous period;

- payments due to suppliers (creditors) incurred in the previous period;

- payments due from customers (debtors) owing from the previous period, and adjustments for bad debts;

- ongoing credit being given and received during the year;

- receipts of loan income or capital;

- capital purchases, lease payments, loan repayments etc.

- in the case of sole traders and partnerships, the income tax liability for the business in the previous year, and with limited companies, the corporation tax liability for the previous period.

Again, as with budgets, cash flow forecasts always exclude VAT charged on sales or paid on purchases. This is because VAT is seen as a positive influence on cash flow, in that all payments are offset against receipts and the balance paid to HM Customs and Excise quarterly in arrears, so that the balance due is collected before it has to be paid out. In theory then, VAT's short-term residence in the trader's bank account should improve cash flow temporarily.

So, why do we bother with cash flow forecasting? The answer quite simply, is solvency, i.e. ensuring that the business can pay its bills and settle its liabilities as and when they fall due. Unless that is the case, the business may be insolvent and, if so, it cannot legally continue to trade, unless steps are taken promptly to redress the insolvency situation. As is explained in Chapter 8, one of the biggest reasons for failure amongst small firms is lack of working capital and, irrespective of how profitable they might be, if they cannot pay their bills, they often go bankrupt or into liquidation.

What then, are the main influences on cash flow? I find that the best way to understand cash flow is to picture working capital as a bucket with holes in it. Cash receipts pour in through the top, and leak out as expenditure through the holes in the bottom. There are ways in which the rate of flow can be increased to top up the level in the bucket, and there are factors that cause a faster outflow, thus reducing the level of working capital in the bucket:

- Increased profits or net receipts from trading improve working capital.

- Receipts of loans or capital investment increase working capital.

- Sale of fixed assets (e.g. land and buildings) or investments releases cash.

- Reduction of stock levels can free cash previously tied up.

- By decreasing debtors (collecting money more quickly or giving less credit) or by increasing creditors (obtaining extra credit or paying late) it is possible to improve cash flow and levels of working capital.

- Conversely, increasing debtors (giving longer credit to customers or taking on more credit customers) and decreasing creditors (paying suppliers quicker) will adversely affect cash flow, reducing the level of available working capital.

- Similarly, repayment of loans, redemption of capital, reduces available cash and working capital. Payment of dividends, profit shares and taxation, have a similar effect in reducing available cash.

- Increasing stock levels ties up cash, and often the increased stock-holding is a response to expansion, which if coupled with an increase in credit customers can reduce available working capital, quite severely.

- Purchase of fixed assets and investments also takes money out of the system. Fixed (long-term) assets need to be financed by long-term liabilities such as loans or mortgages, not by using working capital which is a current (short-term) asset and which is there to fund day-to-day expenditure.

The structure of the cash flow forecast spreadsheet is broadly the same as that of the budget, with the exception of the bottom line. This is an additional line below the net income/expenditure line, which shows the cumulative effect of income and expenditure on cash flow. The basic rule of thumb is that the biggest cumulative deficit figure is the absolute minimum overdraft requirement for the period. If you bear in mind that the cumulative figures represent the roll-up for the month as a

Figure 6.2 Winston Wight cash flow forecast

Item	Jan.	Feb.	March	April	May	June	July	August	Sept.	Oct.	Nov.	Dec.	Totals
INCOME:													
Market stall	£9,000	£12,000	£7,000	£9,000	£8,000	£10,000	£9,000	£8,000	£10,000	£11,000	£15,000	£17,000	£125,000
Non-trading income	£50	£50	£50	£50	£50	£50	£50	£50	£50	£50	£50	£50	£600
Cash balance b/fwd	£9,800	–	–	–	–	–	–	–	–	–	–	–	£9,800
Total Income	£18,850	£12,050	£7,050	£9,050	£8,050	£10,050	£9,050	£8,050	£10,050	£11,050	£15,050	£17,050	£135,400
EXPENDITURE:													
Stall rent	£750	£600	£600	£750	£600	£600	£750	£600	£600	£750	£600	£600	£7,800
Stall wages	£500	£500	£400	£500	£400	£400	£500	£400	£400	£500	£400	£600	£5,500
Stall stock	£7,700	£6,300	£5,700	£4,800	£5,100	£5,400	£5,700	£5,100	£5,400	£6,300	£7,800	£9,600	£74,900
Bags and wrappings	£90	£120	£70	£90	£80	£100	£90	£80	£100	£110	£150	£170	£1,250
Stall fittings	–	–	£50	–	–	–	–	–	£50	–	–	–	£100
Bookkeeper	£30	£30	£30	£30	£30	£30	£30	£30	£30	£30	£30	£30	£360
Admin and expenses	£100	£80	£80	£100	£80	£80	£100	£80	£80	£100	£80	£80	£1,040
Advertising	£30	£60	£30	£30	£30	£30	£30	£30	£30	£30	£30	£60	£420
Insurance	£50	£50	£50	£50	£50	£50	£50	£50	£50	£50	£50	£50	£600
Transport – running costs	£250	£250	£250	£250	£250	£250	£250	£250	£250	£250	£250	£250	£3,000
Transport – hire purchase	£150	£150	£150	£150	£150	£150	£150	£150	£150	£150	£150	£150	£1,800
Bank loan repayments	£100	£100	£100	£100	£100	£100	£100	£100	£100	£100	£100	£100	£1,200
Bank charges	–	–	£300	–	–	£250	–	–	£250	–	–	£250	£1,050
Tax liability previous year	£3,200	–	–	–	–	–	£3,200	–	–	–	–	–	£6,400
Personal drawings	£1,500	£1,200	£1,200	£1,500	£1,200	£1,200	£1,500	£1,200	£1,200	£1,500	£1,200	£1,200	£15,600
Transfer to pension fund	–	–	£1,500	–	–	–	–	–	£1,500	–	–	–	£3,000
Total Expenditure:	£14,450	£9,440	£10,510	£8,350	£8,070	£8,640	£12,450	£8,070	£10,190	£9,870	£10,840	£13,140	£124,020
NET INCOME	£4,400	£2,610	£–3,460	£700	£–20	£1,410	£–3,400	£–20	£–140	£1,180	£4,210	£3,910	£11,380
Cumulative cash-flow	£4,400	£7,010	£3,550	£4,250	£4,230	£5,640	£2,240	£2,220	£2,080	£3,260	£7,470	£11,380	

	£	£
Sales income	125,000	
Non-trading income	600	
Total income		125,600
Stock purchases	75,000	
Plus opening stock	3,000	
	78,000	
Less closing stock	3,000	
Cost of goods sold		75,000
Gross Profit		**50,600**
Less expenses:		
– Stall rent	7,800	
– Bags and wrappings	1,250	
– Stall fittings	100	
– Wages	5,500	
– Book-keeper	360	
– Admin and expenses	1,040	
– Advertising	420	
– Insurance	600	
– Transport running costs	3,000	
– Bank charges	1,050	
– Loan interest	300	
– Hire purchase interest	600	
Total expenses:		22,020
Net Profit Before Tax		**28,580**
Estimated Tax/NIC liability		5,800
Net Profit After Tax		**22,780**
Hire purchase capital repayments	1,200	
Loan capital repayments	900	
Personal drawings	15,600	
Lump sum pension payments	3,000	
Total payments from after-tax profit		20,700
Profit retained in business		**2,080**

Figure 6.3 Winston Wight profit forecast

**Case
Study**

Winston Wight

In Figure 6.1 we saw Winston's budget for the coming year. Figure 6.2 shows the same figures adjusted as a cash flow forecast. Instead of showing when income and expenditure was incurred, this spreadsheet is concerned with the periods in which the money was actually received or paid. It shows the sales revenue, the tax liabilities and dates due, the payments to be made in each month (Winston gets thirty days' credit on 50 per cent of his purchases), the net cash income or expenditure for the month and finally, at the bottom, the cumulative cash balance for the month. It also shows the money which he intends to draw from the business out of his after tax profits, to make lump sum payments into his personal pension fund. These, again, are not trading transactions but do represent a substantial movement of cash out of the business. Note the variations in the monthly net income figures for the two spreadsheets, which illustrates just how different the budgeting and cash flow forecasting processes are from each other.

---

whole, there may be times within the month when, due to late payment by customers and creditor bills falling due, the actual deficit is higher than that shown by the cash flow forecast. Beware, as Murphy's Second Universal Law of Cock-Ups states that your customers will always pay you late when you need it most. So it pays you to build some contingencies into the overdraft requirement, as not only do bank managers tend to worry about requests for repeated increases in overdraft facilities, they charge you extra fees for arranging them.

**The profit
(or loss)
forecast**

The two primary accounting statements that are produced at the end of the financial year are the balance sheet and the profit and loss account. The balance sheet is like a snapshot taken at

---

Winston Wight

Figure 6.3 shows the profit forecast for Winston Wight's market stall. As can be seen, many of the financial sums have been taken straight from the totals column of Winston's budgetary plan (Figure 6.1); but it is the points of difference that we are interested in:

- Winston's personal drawings are excluded from expenses section of the profit forecast as these are taken out of the net profit after tax. As a sole trader he pays income tax and Class 4 NIC on the profits of the business, and not on his personal drawings.

- Loan repayments are also paid out of net profit after tax, only the interest payable on the loan counts as a business expense which can be set against profits. Winston has to obtain a certificate of interest paid, from his bank, to verify the figures.

- Similarly, the capital part of hire purchase payments is claimed as a capital allowance for tax purposes, so capital payments are paid out of net profit after tax, but the interest does count as an operating expense. Winston's hire purchase agreement specifies the total interest payable over the period of the contract.

---

the final moment of the financial year. It shows the resources which have been put into the company by the owners or investors, any long-term borrowing (capital and liabilities), and the way in which those resources have been deployed (assets) e.g. in the form of land, buildings, machinery, cash, stock, etc. In contrast, the profit and loss account for the financial year acts as a summary of the trading and profitability of the business over the year as a whole. The reason these two statements are read together is quite simple. Whilst the balance sheet tells us all about the assets, capital and liabilities of the business, it tells us nothing about the profitability. Conversely, the profit and loss account tells us all about the profitability and efficiency of trading over the year, but it shows us nothing of the assets and liabilities.

As stated above, the profit and loss account is a historical record prepared at the end of the year, but the profit forecast, which ideally follows the same format for ease of comparison, is prepared at the same time as the budgetary plan and cash flow forecast. In fact, much of the information for the profit forecast will be drawn from the 'Totals' column of the budgetary plan.

In summary, we have examined the five main forecasts which would be expected to be included in a business plan: the personal survival budget, the breakeven analysis, the annual budgetary plan, the cash flow forecast and the profit forecast. It may be however, that depending on your circumstances you would not actually need all of these in your own business plan. For example, a non-profit-making organization by definition would not need a profit forecast, but it still needs to know if it is breaking even. Someone working part-time on a self-employed basis may only need a simple budget, and if working for cash, this could also form the cash flow forecast. The important factor is that you need to know how these documents work and what they are used for in order to decide whether or not they are relevant to your own particular business plan. If you are an NVQ candidate, you need to be able to show that you understand the documents in order to satisfy the underpinning knowledge requirements of the NVQ Unit A4. Most important of all, you need to understand them in order to use them to monitor and control the growth and development of your business.

Further reading

Izhar, R. (1994). *Accounting, Costing and Management*. Oxford University Press.

Mason, R. (1993). *Finance for Non-Financial Managers in a Week*. IoM and Headway.

Secrett, M. (1993). *Mastering Spreadsheet Budgets and Forecasts*. Pitman and IoM.

Sizer, D. (1997). *An Insight into Management Accounting*. Penguin.

Chapter 7   Financial controls

Chapter 7   controls
Chapter 7

Chapter 7 links closely with the preceding chapter and is concerned with monitoring and controlling the financial performance of the business. The objective of this chapter is to provide a practical understanding of some of the basic methods of maintaining financial controls, and of some of the simple techniques used for assessing financial performance, in order to make the reader aware of how these can be employed to the benefit of the business. These will include:

- basic accounts and double-entry book-keeping;

- monitoring budgets and cash flow;

- profit margins and mark-up;

- stock control;

- aged debtors accounts;

- credit control procedures;

- accounting ratios.

For the NVQ candidate, this chapter corresponds with Elements 4.3 and 4.4 of the NVQ Level 3, Business Planning, which focus on the accounting processes and financial monitoring and control requirements of a small business. The evidence requirements overlap with those described in the previous chapter, but the emphasis is less on forecasting and more on monitoring the ongoing progress, by comparing the forecasts with actual achievement. In order to do this, the candidate requires the basic underpinning knowledge of how accounting systems work, and how financial performance can be assessed.

It is a legal requirement for any business, charity, trust, voluntary organization, public body etc., to maintain a true and accurate record of its financial transactions. For tax purposes, these accounts have to be retained for a period of six years. Accounts are prepared on a yearly basis and, depending on the size and turnover of the business, can be completed in one of two ways. For businesses with a turnover below £350 000, accounting can be carried out on a cash basis, whereby the financial transactions are recorded only when money actually changes hands, i.e. when payments are made or received. Where the turnover exceeds that figure then the VAT regulations require that accounting is carried out on a commitment basis, whereby the transaction has to be recorded as soon as any goods or services are supplied or received, irrespective of the subsequent date of payment.

Basic account-ing and double-entry book-keeping

Double-entry book-keeping works on the principle that when a sales or purchase transaction is entered in the appropriate ledger column of the accounts, a corresponding entry is made in the cash or bank columns to show where payments were made from, or into which accounts any receipts were paid. If this process is carefully maintained, it provides an easy way of reconciling the accounts with bank statements and petty cash. Figure 7.1 shows an example of a simple double-entry accounts sheet suitable for a small business operating on a cash accounting basis. The number of sales and purchase column headings can be expanded to suit the needs of the business, and analysis books with varying numbers of such columns are readily available from high street stationers.

Date	Item	Cash In	Cash Out	Bank In	Bank Out	Rent & Rates	Resale Stock	Transport	Admin & Expense	Wages & Drawings	Sales & Adverts	VAT on Inputs	Total Purchase	Sales Revenue	VAT on Outputs	Total Income
1/5/00	Balance b/fwd	852.17		1,972.83		430.00	5,120.00	152.25	33.48	2,220.00	15.00	929.47	8,900.20	7,741.50	1,354.76	9,096.26
3/5/00	Rent		300.00		300.00	300.00							300.00			
4/5/00	Petrol		23.50					20.00				3.50	23.50			
4/5/00	Stock purchases				1,527.50		1,300.00					227.50	1,527.50			
4/5/00	Expenses		28.00						25.20			2.80	28.00			
7/5/00	Wages		180.00							180.00			180.00			
7/5/00	Sales w/e	258.92		2,000.00										1,922.49	336.43	2,258.92
10/5/00	Telephone bill				262.35				223.28			39.07	262.35			
11/5/00	Van repair				235.00			200.00				35.00	235.00			
11/5/00	Stock purchases				1,386.50		1,180.00					206.50	1,386.50			
12/5/00	Petrol		35.25					30.00				5.25	35.25			
13/5/00	Newspaper ad				17.63						15.00	2.63	17.63			
14/5/00	Wages		180.00							180.00			180.00			
14/5/00	Sales w/e	253.52		1,950.00										1,875.34	328.18	2,203.52
17/5/00	Stock purchases				1,433.50		1,220.00					213.50	1,433.50			
18/5/00	Expenses		19.57						17.47			2.10	19.57			
19/5/00	Rates				130.00	130.00							130.00			
21/5/00	Wages		180.00							180.00			180.00			
23/5/00	Sales w/e	200.80		1,900.00										1,787.92	312.88	2,100.80
24/5/00	Petrol		35.25					30.00				5.25	35.25			
24/5/00	Stock purchases				1,586.25		1,350.00					236.25	1,586.25			
28/5/00	Stationery		11.75						10.00			1.75	11.75			
28/5/00	Wages		180.00							180.00			180.00			
30/5/00	Sales w/e	154.98		2,250.00										2,046.79	358.19	2404.98
30/5/00	Drawings		150.00		1,350.00					1,500.00			1,500.00			
31/5/00	Balance c/fwd	£697.07		1,844.10		860.00	10,170.00	432.25	309.43	4,440.00	30.00	1,910.57	18,152.25	15,374.04	2,690.44	18,064.48

Figure 7.1 Double-entry book-keeping

As the accounting process becomes more complex, i.e. where credit is given for goods and services sold, and received from the business' own suppliers, then the system will need to be more detailed. For example it will be necessary to differentiate between those entries which are paid and those which are still outstanding, and the dates when the payments were made or received. For a newly established business the paper-based system may be adequate in the early stages, but there comes a point (typically around 120–150 transactions per month), when handwritten ledgers are no longer cost-effective and a computerized system is required. These are now available quite cheaply, and are relatively easy to install and operate. They offer the added benefits of integrating the various component parts of the system. For example, the production of invoices is linked with entries in the sales ledger and the stock control systems. Similarly, payroll systems, stock control and purchase orders can be linked to purchase ledgers. The various components of the system are usually integrated via a nominal ledger which is used to produce monthly budget outturn reports, monthly debtors and creditors analysis, etc., and the annual balance sheet and profit and loss account at the end of the financial year. These provide accurate and up-to-date information which is invaluable in monitoring and controlling the finances of the business, and which is much harder and more time-consuming to extract from a manual accounting system.

Monitoring budgets and cash flow

Chapter 6 explained in detail the importance of producing detailed cash flow forecasts and budgetary plans, but apart from keeping the bank manager quiet for a while, these are of little value to the business if they are not monitored on a regular basis. At least once a month, and preferably as soon as possible after the end of each month, the actual sales volumes and revenues, and the actual expenditure incurred in each area within the business, needs to be compared with the forecast figures to identify any significant discrepancies. Where such discrepancies occur, they need to be analysed to determine the cause, and to identify whether or not they constitute a one-off situation or part of a developing trend which might adversely affect the longer-term prospects of the business. Having identified them, it is then necessary to assess the impact that that they will make on business operations and profit. If the budgetary plan has been prepared on a computerized spreadsheet, this is a relatively simple process, as the actual data can be entered into a copy of the original budget to produce revised outturn figures.

This process is even more important when forecasting cash flow, as relatively small changes in sales revenue or credit terms can, over a period of time, compound themselves to create a major cash flow problem. However if the problems can be spotted in time, then it is often possible to address those problems before they become too great, e.g. by arranging a short-term overdraft, by tightening credit limits or the length of credit given to customers or by extending the credit received from suppliers, although ideally they should be consulted first.

Profit margins and mark-up

This is a topic which many people who are relatively new to business find hard to comprehend. When we talk of *profit margin* we mean the difference between the selling price and the cost price. If we buy an item for £60 and sell it for £100 the profit margin is £40 which constitutes 40 per cent of the selling price. When we talk of *mark-up* we mean the amount or percentage by which the cost price is increased to produce the selling price. Using the same example, if we buy an item for £60 and mark it up by £40, it will sell for £100, but the mark-up as a percentage of the cost price is 66.7 per cent. Similarly, a 100 per cent mark-up gives 50 per cent profit margin, a 50 per cent mark-up gives 33 per cent profit margin, a 33 per cent mark-up gives a 25 per cent profit margin, and a 25 per cent mark-up gives a 20 per cent profit margin.

Failing to distinguish between these two terms is probably the commonest and most significant mistake made by people who are new to business. The anticipated 50 per cent gross profit was in reality only 33 per cent and, with a few unexpected expenses, some increased costs during the year and a small drop in sales revenue, the forecast 10 per cent net profit on sales turnover has suddenly become a 15 per cent net loss, and there is no spare cash to pay the bills that are due next week! There is little detailed published data on reasons for small business failure and bankruptcy, but I would seriously contend that this all too familiar scenario is probably one of the primary reasons why many emerging small businesses fail to survive beyond their first or second year.

Stock control

For providers of services, where the only stock which is held is likely to consist of stationery or consumables, then stock control will probably not cause any major problems, but for manufacturers, wholesalers and retailers the situation can be totally different. Stock-related problems can include:

- Having inadequate volumes of raw materials to produce goods.

- Having inadequate volumes of completed goods to meet sales orders.

- Having the wrong types of goods in stock.

- Having too much money tied up in slow-moving stock, causing cash flow problems.

- Being unable to obtain stock from suppliers (particularly imported goods) on a regular or reliable basis.

- Having to handle a high proportion of returns of faulty or unsatisfactory stock.

- Being left with unsaleable or outdated goods.

- Careless storage or handling resulting in damaged stock.

- Inaccurate invoicing of stock sold, or poor stock control resulting in inaccurate stock records.

- Theft of stock, or slippage (e.g. removal of stock by staff for own use).

Most of the above problems are fundamentally concerned with operational issues relating to the ordering processes, and the physical storage and stock management systems used by the business; however, all of these will have an impact on the profit margins which the business makes. Stock levels need to monitored carefully to ensure that they are adequate to meet foreseeable demand but without tying up cash unnecessarily for long periods of time. This will involve both regular liaison will sales and marketing staff to assess future levels of demand, and an efficient system of ordering replacement stock, e.g. by identifying both minimal acceptable levels of stock, and levels at which new stock must be ordered allowing for lead times for delivery etc. It is no good waiting until the stock reaches the minimum level before reordering, if that stock is likely to run out before the delivery is received. If the delivery takes two weeks to arrive, then the reorder level must be set at the minimum stock level plus the amount of stock that would typically be utilized during that two week lead time. Many larger organizations, particularly in the automotive industry, now use 'just in time' ordering and stock delivery systems where stock can be ordered and delivered at short notice. This works well for them as it saves them the expense of holding large quantities of stock, but it often results in their smaller suppliers having to bear the cost of holding that stock on their behalf.

Whilst the physical monitoring of stock is important to detect any theft, damage resulting from storage or handling and deterioration due to poor stock rotation, it is also important to monitor the financial aspects of stock control. Wholesalers and retailers who handle a large number of stock lines have to deal with a constant stream of changing prices, discount structures, special promotions etc., all of which affect the purchase price of each of the stock lines. Unless these ever changing costs are checked on a regular basis (ideally on the receipt of each purchase invoice) then profit margins can unknowingly become eroded. The larger the range of stock lines, the more important it is to use some form of database or financial stock control system to record the cost prices, profit margins, and selling prices, and to flag up any changes in the purchase price of goods.

It is also useful to monitor the rate at which stock is being turned over. For example, if I hold an average of £10 000 of stock and make an average level of sales of £60 000 per month, then I am effectively turning that stock around six times per month, or every five days, which means that I am making excellent use of my working capital. If on the other hand, I am holding the same level of stock but only selling £20 000 per month, then I am only turning the stock over once every fifteen days. I am probably holding more in stock than I really need, which means that I have too much money tied up in stock, and I am not making the best use of my working capital. Obviously the ideal turnover rate will vary from one industry to another, but the basic principle remains the same.

At the end of each financial year (and frequently at the half-year stage) it is necessary to carry out a full and detailed inventory of all items of stock, and to determine the full value of the stock (at cost). Annual stocktaking forms part of the process of preparing the annual balance sheet of the business, and there are a number of ways in which the stock values can be calculated. Under the last in first out (LIFO) method, stock is valued at the price pertaining to the oldest items held, which can be a complicated process if stock has been received at different prices over a period of time. Under the first in first out (FIFO) method, stock is valued at the latest price, which presents an easier method of calculation but with the risk of overvaluing the stock, particularly if much of it is old. A more practical and realistic method is to divide the total value of all items of stock by the number of units, giving what is called a 'weighted average cost', which reflects the true value of each line of stock. It is important to remember that the choice of method of valuation will influence the cost of goods sold in the profit and loss account, which in turn will affect the gross profit calculations and, subsequently, the taxable profit of the business.

Aged debtors and creditors accounts

These are simple monthly reports which are readily available from computerized accounting systems, but which unfortunately many small businesses overlook unless prompted to produce them by their bank manager. They certainly do require more effort to produce from a manual accounting system, but in either case, if credit facilities are given to customers or received from suppliers on a regular basis, these are essential.

The aged debtors analysis, an example of which is shown in Figure 7.2, is used to assess the performance of customers in paying their bills (and the performance of the business in collecting the debts). The aged creditors analysis is virtually identical in structure but it is used to measure the performance of the business in paying its debts to its own suppliers, the creditors. In the aged debtors analysis, each unpaid invoice for each credit customer is allocated to the thirty-day period in which it was issued. Let us take, for example, the fairly standard business credit terms wherein payment is required within thirty days of the end of the month in which the invoice was issued. Any invoices issued this month are not yet due, and are regarded as current. Those falling due at the end of next month are classed as nought to thirty days old, and are within the terms of credit. Those which are thirty to sixty days old should have been paid by now, and so are in need of chasing. Those which are sixty to ninety days old are of major concern and, unless they are part of an ongoing dispute, must be regarded as being at risk, or in accountancy terms they are a 'doubtful debt'. The ninety days plus category is a definite sign of a bad debt, and debt recovery action should have been taken long ago. One of the basic

Customer	Current £	1–30 days £	31–60 days ££	61–90 days £	91+ days £	Total debt £
Winston Wight	462.00	1,150.50	981.70	–	–	2,594.20
Helen Highwater Associates	112.80	534.60	–	–	–	647.40
Grabbit & Runn, Solicitors	227.90	722.50	847.10	693.30	–	2,490.80
Rojjers & Ammerstein	350.20	211.00	–	–		561.20
W & H Clinton Ltd	–	–	987.50	675.80	992.30	2,655.60
Evan Elpus & Partners	–	125.70	–	–	–	125.70
Ben Dover & Sons	1,349.20	1,878.10	–	–	–	3,227.30
Lemmon & McArthney Ltd	484.00	525.50	293.90	–	–	1,303.40
Totals	2,986.10	5,147.90	3,110.20	1,369.10	992.30	13,605.60
Percentage of total debtors	21.95	37.84	22.86	10.06	7.29	100.00

Figure 7.2 Aged debtors analysis example

principles of accounting, the Prudence Concept, requires that profits are not classed as such until they are in cash or near cash form. Similarly, any doubtful or bad debts must be acknowledged as such at the earliest opportunity. If nothing else, then at least by acknowledging the post ninety-day debts as bad, if you have taken recovery action then you can claim bad debt relief for them when making the next VAT return, although if the debt is eventually settled, then that relief will have to be repaid.

Credit control procedures

So, it is becoming obvious that some of your customers do not want to pay you, or cannot pay you, then what can you do about it? There are a number of options available:

- Send in a few big lads, the heavy mob, armed with baseball bats to break a few bones. Very popular in certain Mediterranean countries, but strictly illegal, and there is always the risk that their lads might just be a bit bigger than yours! Not exactly the best or first choice option for a respectable growing business.

- Telephone or send a reminder letter. Why not try? After all, the non-payment may simply be the result of an oversight. However, if the customer is a serial bad payer this is likely to have no effect at all, as reminders will simply be ignored.

- If no further response within seven to fourteen days, then try again and preferably more firmly. Contact the decision maker or person responsible for payment. Check that the payment is not in dispute. Ask outright if there is a cash flow problem and ask for a firm date by which payment (or at least part payment) can be expected. Again, the serial bad payer will probably just make empty promises at this stage, and will stretch their credit to the limit until forced to pay. There are, unfortunately, still a few people in business who regard this process as being one big game.

- Once the payment becomes thirty days overdue, then unless there are special circumstances that you are prepared to accept, or unless you have negotiated an agreement for repayment, then you must seriously consider stopping further supplies. Some small firms find this a hard step to take, as they run the risk of the customer going to another supplier. So what! A sale is not a sale until it is paid for, and if the customer is slow in paying you, then the same will probably apply to their next supplier, and you will be better off without them in the long term. It may come as a surprise to you, but some customers even respect this firm approach.

- If the customer is in difficulty, then you may be able to negotiate a structured programme of repayment without a loss of trade. I have found this to work on may occasions where, for example, the customer pays cash on delivery for the regular weekly supply of goods plus an agreed minimum figure to reduce the outstanding balance. Very often this forms the basis for a future long-term trading relationships, as once the customers had overcome the current problems then they remain loyal to the suppliers who had worked with them during the difficult period. But if you do agree to take this route, you must not allow the outstanding balance to increase at any stage until the debt has been cleared and normal trading terms have been re-established.

- Once you get beyond the ninety-day stage, there is little option but to take formal debt recovery action. Most owner-managers are very busy people, and have little time to pursue bad payers. Solicitors are one alternative, although expensive to employ and often laboriously slow to get results. Professional debt collection agencies are often a better alternative as, apart from an initial assignment fee and the reimbursement of their legal expenses, they work on the basis of taking an agreed percentage of the money they recover. They also tend to tell you up front when faced by a hopeless situation, whereas a solicitor might run up expensive bills before reaching the same conclusion.

- For sums under £3 000 the Small Claims Court is supposed to offer a quick and inexpensive form of redress, without involving solicitors. However, the sheer volume of small claims with which they deal means that the process can still take some months, even if uncontested. The downside is that if your customer lives at a distance from yourself, the court action will often end up being transferred to the defendants local County Court, leaving you with the cost and burden of travelling to their locality. For larger debts it is possible to take action by means of issuing a High Court writ against the debtor, although the cost of doing so is quite high. The High Court tends to move faster than the County Court, particularly when applications are made for compulsory winding-up orders; but once again, the cost of action must be measured against the likelihood of recovering the debt.

- As part of the Insolvency Act 1986 the facility was created to issue a statutory demand for payment, whereby if payment for a debt was not made within twenty-one days of the issue of the statutory demand, then the plaintiff could automatically apply for the business to be wound up or declared bankrupt. This is fine in principle if the business has any assets that could be liquidated in the event of bankruptcy, although if that were the case, then the company could probably raise the money to pay the bill anyway. If there are no tangible assets against which to claim, the pursuants of the claim could simply be incurring more legal expenses only to find themselves alongside a whole host of other unsecured creditors.

● Where goods are supplied to customers it is possible to write the terms of trade which appear on the reverse side of business invoices to include retention of title to the goods supplied, until such times as full payment is made for them. The owner then has the right to reclaim the goods if payment is not made, although this does not confer rights of entry to premises to recover them, neither does it help if the goods have already been sold. This can sometimes be of use when goods are confiscated by bailiffs or receivers in bankruptcy, as those goods cannot subsequently be sold, and will have to be returned to the supplier once proof of title has been demonstrated.

**Account-
ing ratios**   These are not so much methods of monitoring and controlling business finances, as tools which can be used to assess the performance of the business, particularly in terms of solvency and liquidity. There are a host of ratios that can be applied to test business performance, but we will concentrate on a few which are of significance to the small business:

1   The working capital ratio (also called the current ratio) tests the short-term liquidity of a business. It compares the current assets (cash, stock, debtors and work in progress) to the current liabilities (bills falling due for

137

payment). Ideally the current assets:current liability ratio should be 2:1. If the ratio is less, then stock levels or credit facilities given to customers may be too high.

2   The liquidity ratio (or acid test) is a more precise measure of liquidity, as it compares the liquid assets of the business (current assets less slow-moving stock or bad debts) with the current liabilities. Here the liquid assets:current liabilities ratio should be at least 1:1 to demonstrate that the business can meet its current obligations.

3   The gearing ratio is more concerned with solvency, as it compares the equity (or share capital) and reserves of the business with its long-term borrowings, to ensure that loans etc. can be repaid if the business should cease trading. It is regarded as a good measure of the borrowing capacity of the business, as the higher the ratio, the better the borrowing potential.

4   The asset cover ratio compares total assets with total debt to determine how many times the debts of the business are covered by its assets. This again reflects the borrowing capacity of the business, as the higher the ratio, the more it is likely to be able to borrow.

5   The return on capital employed (ROCE) ratio compares the profit received from ordinary trading activities before interest, with the sum of the capital employed in trading. It is expressed as a percentage. For example, if the company employs capital of £100 000 and produces a profit from ordinary trading of £30 000 it has made an (ROCE) of 30 per cent. This ratio is of key interest to potential investors. It is also important to remember that if the ratio falls below the average level of interest paid on bank deposits or investments, then the business would be better off not trading, and just leaving its capital on deposit at the bank.

6   Finally the sales: working capital (current assets less current liabilities) ratio tests the number of times the

working capital is being utilized each year. Like the sales revenue:average stock ratio described in the 'Stock control' section of this chapter, the sales:working capital ration is a measure of how well the business is using its resources.

In summarizing this chapter, it must be emphasized that the effective monitoring and control of finances involves the use of a whole range of tools and techniques on a regular ongoing basis. Moreover, those tools and techniques complement each other and are best used alongside each other rather than in isolation.

Chapter 8 Sources
Chapter 8 of finance
Chapter 8

The chances are that unless you win the National Lottery, inherit a fortune, marry a rich widow or toy boy or find a sugar daddy, that you will sooner or later have to raise some short-term or long-term finance for your business. The most obvious source of funding for most owner-managers is from the local high street bank, but this is not necessarily the cheapest or best way of financing a particular borrowing requirement.

The purpose of this chapter is to examine some of the potential sources of finance that are available for new and expanding businesses, and to examine their relative uses, advantages and disadvantages. For the NVQ candidate, Element 4.2 'Identify how the business will be funded' requires the candidate to demonstrate that various funding options have been examined and appropriate choices made, and that these can be fully justified.

In many cases this will involve considering not just the finance required for the initial start-up phase of the business to cover the period until the firm achieve regular profitable trading. It is just as important to consider and identify the available options for the next stage, when the firm starts to expand, possibly at a rate which is faster than receipts from profits can support. The effective planning of finance at this stage is critical to avoid over-trading, where the business is growing beyond the level which can be supported by its own working capital. This is one of the most common causes of business failure, when growth outstrips working capital and results in a cash flow crisis and inability to pay suppliers, wages etc. on time. In this situation, profits might be excellent, but the firm is still technically insolvent and, therefore, trading illegally. Some firms manage to hang on and trade out of this situation but, for the majority, the only sensible remedy is to raise finance to increase working capital to a level that will support the expansion.

Factors which influence suitable sources of finance

The most appropriate form of borrowing will be determined by a number of factors:

- *The purpose for which the funds are required*, e.g. whether it is to increase working capital, or to acquire a vehicle or an item of capital equipment. For the former, a medium-term loan would be suitable, whereas for vehicles or plant and equipment, leasing or hire purchase might be better.

- *The size of the borrowing requirement.* Most bankers will only lend against security. A personal guarantee may be adequate for a few thousand pounds, but for a more substantial sum the loan will need to be secured by a legal charge on property. Borrowing small sums can also be quite expensive in that interest rates tend to fall as the size of loan increases and, with small loans, the initial set up fees form a larger proportion of the total cost.

- *The anticipated repayment period.* Short-term borrowing tends to incur higher rates of interest, whilst the rate usually falls when spread over a longer period. Some forms of finance, such as commercial mortgages, also have maximum repayment periods or repayment periods that are linked to the size of the borrowing, as in the case of car loans.

- *The affordability of repayments.* The crucial question when assessing funding options is 'Can the business afford to make the required regular payments from its current or expected levels of profit?' If not, we must question the viability of the business: 'Is it really worth carrying on?' If so, we must question the necessity of the borrowing: 'Do I really need a new car, or will the current one last another year?' Then, we need to examine the alternative funding options: 'Can I find another lender who will consider lower repayments spread over a longer period?'

- *The availability of security or collateral.* As bankers will rarely lend against the full equity value of property (50 per cent is a more realistic figure for some high street banks), the availability of the loan may be limited by the equity or residual value of the property against which it will be secured. If the net value of your home is £50 000, then you may only be able to borrow £25 000 to £30 000 against it.

These are some of the commonly used options most regularly used by smaller organizations to raise finance.

Equity or capital

This is basically the value of the resources that are introduced into the business by its owners or investors. These resources do not have to be in cash form only, as they can include just about anything of value that will be of positive use to the business, including saleable stock, vehicles, computer equipment, land and buildings, office equipment, plant and machinery etc. In the case of sole traders and partnerships, the value of these resources is assigned to a capital account for each of the proprietors. In a limited company the resources become the property of the company, against which shares are issued. The investors cannot withdraw their capital investment but, if the company wishes and if it can afford to do so, then the company can redeem or buy back the shares from the investors.

Funding options for small and medium-sized businesses

Unsecured loans

Unless you have a long-standing and proven track record, obtaining an unsecured business loan from a bank, for anything but a small sum, is a virtual impossibility. Many small businesses are started with unsecured loans from friends or family, as this can be a very low-cost and flexible way of getting started. However, it is very much in the interests of both lenders and borrowers to in some way formalize the loan arrangements in writing, even if only by means of a covering letter signed by both parties. This would, for example, show details of the lender and borrower, the sum involved and the purpose of the loan, the date borrowed and the date when repayment is due and details of interest payable (or not payable). Even a simple signed document would protect the lender in the case of default by the borrower. Similarly, if say the lender died, then the deceased's estate could not demand immediate repayment of the loan prior to the agreed date.

Overdrafts

Overdrafts are essentially a short-term form of borrowing, designed to cover temporary periods when cash flow may be poor, or during seasonal troughs such as those experienced in the coastal holiday trade. These are usually only granted for up to one year, and approval and reapproval incurs an arrangement fee charged by the lender. Interest rates are quite high, but interest is only charged when the overdraft facility is in use. The important thing to remember, is that if you find that you need a permanent overdraft, then you do not need an overdraft at all. What you really need is a longer-term loan.

Loan guarantee schemes

These schemes were introduced by the government in the early 1980s to encourage banks to lend to new and small firms whose proprietors could not offer any conventional security. The idea was that the government, in return for a percentage charge, would guarantee up to 80 per cent of the value of the loan. The banks, in return for a higher rate of loan interest, would stand the risk of the other 20 per cent. Loan guarantees can still be found, but the scheme as a whole was viewed as an abysmal failure. Apart from the high cost of interest and fees, banks simply do not like to risk lending even as little as 20 per cent for a new business on an unsecured basis, and so were only willing to advance money to established firms with a proven track record. Homeowner applicants were told that as they had potential security, the loan guarantee scheme was inappropriate. Applicants with no assets were asked why the bank should risk backing them when they had nothing at risk themselves.

Short- and medium-term bank loans

These typically involve repayments over two to five years, but sometimes up to seven years. For sums in excess of £5000, security would almost certainly be required in the form of a charge against private or company property, or of a fixed and floating charge over the book debts and assets of the business. For short-term loans for sums below £5000, a personal guarantee of payment in the event of default would probably be acceptable, as long as it was given by one or more persons with tangible assets (e.g. homeowners). Interest would typically be fixed at between 2 per cent and 5 per cent over the base rate prevailing at the time the loan was taken out. The precise rate of interest may be influenced by the type of security offered, in that better security may attract a lower rate of interest. Arrangement fees are also charged on new loans.

Long-term loans from banks

High street banks will make long term loans to businesses, typically over five to ten years on a secured basis. Beyond that period, the loan is more likely to be treated as a mortgage, being secured by a specific fixed asset belonging to the business or one of its proprietors. Again, arrangement fees are charged and there may be some solicitor's costs incurred in setting up legal charges on property.

Share capital from private investors – ordinary shares

Private limited companies cannot offer their shares for sale to the general public, as only those companies listed and quoted on the Stock Exchange or the Alternative Investment Market can do that. However, private limited companies can still sell shares privately to individual investors or to other companies. These transactions normally involve the purchase of a fixed number of ordinary shares for an agreed sum that then belongs to the company. Ordinary shares confer voting rights on the owner, and dividends are paid annually from company profits, usually in the form of so many pence per share.

Share capital from private investors – preference shares

These are sold in the same way as ordinary shares, but are fundamentally different in that ownership of them confers no voting rights and there is normally an option for the issuing company to buy them back (redeem them) after a fixed period of time. In lieu of those rights, preferential shareholders receive guaranteed dividends, which are fixed or have a minimum payment level and which are paid even when no dividends are paid to holders of ordinary shares. If no dividend is paid one year, then the next time that one is declared, the preferential shareholders will receive recompense for any past unpaid dividend. In the event of liquidation, holders of preference shares have priority over ordinary shareholders if any residual funds are available for distribution.

Debentures

Debentures are a special type of fixed-term loan, often guaranteed by a charge on the assets of the business and sometimes linked to an option to convert into share capital. They differ from conventional loans in that during the lifetime of the loan, only interest is paid, as the capital sum does not fall due for repayment until the period of the loan expires, when it must be repaid in full. Interest rates are agreed at the start of the term, either at a fixed level, or linked to commercial lending rates with a minimum specified level. Debentures will often be arranged between one company and another, or by financial institutions, particularly to assist with expansion of a business.

Mortgage debentures

As the name suggests, these are debentures that are mortgaged to a specific fixed asset of the company, e.g. a piece of land or a building. Otherwise they work in the same way as a debenture.

Grants

Grants to assist in the setting up of a new business are quite scarce, although for those who are under twenty-five, it is worth applying to the Prince's Youth Trust which makes grants available to unemployed young people who wish to start up on their own. Some relocation grants are available for businesses starting up or moving to development areas, particularly in remote rural areas. Local authorities in urban redevelopment areas often have access to European Social Fund monies, which are sometimes issued in grant form to assist small firms, and local councils or chambers of commerce can often advise on the availability of these, as they will differ from area to area. Grants to subsidise training for employees can also be obtained from some local authority economic development units, and from most Training and Enterprise Councils, Business Links or Enterprise Agencies, which are shortly to be redesignated under a new title. Up to 50 per cent of the cost of training can currently be obtained by firms working towards Investors in People status.

Commercial mortgages

A person who is buying their own home will normally take out a mortgage with a bank or building society typically over twenty-five to thirty years. A commercial mortgage arranged through a bank, insurance company or financial institution is basically the same, but would normally be repaid over ten to fifteen years. Commercial mortgages for licensed premises can also be obtained from some of the regional and national breweries, linked to a contract to buy their products.

Venture capital

Venture capital organizations are specialist companies that invest in new businesses and unquoted companies to help them expand and grow. Investments can take the form of loans or minority shareholdings, but the majority of these companies will only advance sums exceeding £500 000 so their main area of interest is in expansion rather than business start-up. They are generally looking for investments offering potentially high returns (20–40 per cent of capital investment) from dividends and capital growth to justify the investment risks that they take. They frequently seek boardroom representation, will require regular and detailed reports and information, and will often expect the business in which they have invested to buy out their share after a specified period of time. On the positive side, venture capital companies can provide the levels of investment which might otherwise only be obtainable via the Stock Exchange, but without the massive cost of achieving Stock Exchange listing. They also impose structure and regulation of company affairs. On the negative side, they can restrict the owners' ability to make decisions, their expectations are high and the owner loses a good deal of strategic control over the business. The owner will also be liable for legal and accountancy charges to facilitate the capital injection.

Hire purchase

This is usually used to buy a fixed asset such as a vehicle or piece of plant or machinery. Under a hire purchase agreement, the business would typically pay 20 per cent of the cost of the asset plus the full VAT sum up front, with the hire purchase company financing the balance. The VAT is claimed back at the next quarter, and fixed monthly payments are then made over a specific period of time, perhaps three to five years, at the end of which the asset belongs to the business. In case of default on monthly payments, the hire purchase company, which still technically owns the asset until the final payment is made, can recover and sell the asset. If the business has already paid at least two-thirds of the money due, then recovery will require a court order. Hire purchase is useful to a business that wants to show the fixed asset on its balance sheet, however, being a capital purchase, capital allowance taxation rules apply.

Leasing or contract hire

In the case of hire purchase, the asset eventually becomes the property of the business, but with lease hire or contract hire this transfer of ownership does not occur. The business simply makes regular monthly payments to the leasing company over the duration of the contract, and has the use of the asset during that time. Leasing is cheaper to set up, usually requiring an initial deposit of only three months' payments, with VAT being charged on each payment. Leasing is good for cash flow, and is tax-effective as all payments count as a business expense, but as ownership of the asset never changes hands, it cannot be included in the company balance sheet.

Factoring or invoice discounting

Factoring involves the management of the firm's sales ledger by an outside organization, typically a bank. First, all company customers are given a very tight and careful credit check and, when approved, the factoring company guarantees to pay the business a fixed percentage (e.g. up to 80 per cent) of the value of every invoice within fourteen days of the issue of the invoice. The balance, less a factoring charge, is paid once the debt has been settled. The system is excellent for cash flow, but factoring companies are very strict and can be heavy-handed in dealing with customers, which may result in the loss of trade. There is also usually a minimum turnover requirement of £250 000, so the system is hardly suitable for new or start-up businesses. Invoice discounting works in a similar way, but the sales ledger is controlled by the company itself, with advances of up to 80 per cent being made against specific invoices. The company repays the advance when the debt is collected, and interest is paid at between 2 per cent and 5 per cent over normal commercial rates.

These are mentioned in passing, just to draw the reader's attention to the fact that they exist, as they would certainly not be relevant to most small firms. Taking those firms at the top end of the government's definition of 'small and medium-sized enterprises' which employ between 100 and 250 staff, some of those would be more likely to consider using the following options. However, for the 87 per cent of firms in the UK which only employ less than twenty staff, they are largely inappropriate.

Further funding options more suited to larger organizations

Commercial bonds

These are way out of the league of small firms, as commercial bonds usually are issued by large blue-chip companies. The company issues (sells) a negotiable bond with a guaranteed redemption value of perhaps £100 000 payable in five or ten years' time. The initial selling price is less than the face value but, as time progresses towards the redemption date, the value will increase. Dealings in the bonds take place on the Stock Exchange.

Bills of exchange

Usually with a value of at least £100 000, these are a bit like post-dated cheques, but they are only payable when certain conditions have been met, e.g. the goods to which the bill of exchange relates have been delivered. However, they can be discounted to finance early payment, or money can be borrowed against them, subject to the reputation and status of the issuing company.

Stock Exchange or Alternative Investment Market flotation

This can be a very expensive process, and is generally regarded as not being justified unless the floating company intends to raise at least £5 million. The company has to prove that it can meet certain accounting, operational and capitalization standards in order to find a merchant bank willing to underwrite the floatation (i.e. to buy up all of the surplus shares if no one else wants to buy them). Once listed, its shares can be sold to the public, and the capital raised can be used for expansion.

Convertible loan stock

This takes the form of an option to buy shares in a company, which is issued against loans from financial institutions or investment companies. The issuing company receives a loan usually at a low interest rate, with no capital repayments until the settlement date and with the interest being paid out of pre-tax earnings, so this amounts to a very cheap form of finance. The lending company, as well as receiving interest on the loan, has an option at the end of the loan period. If the borrowing company's shares have performed poorly, the loan can be repaid in full and the share option returned. Alternatively, if the shares have increased in value in the meantime, the lending company can exercise its right to buy them at the original price in lieu of repayment of the loan, (i.e. 'convert' the loan into shares) and sell them for a capital profit.

Capital reserves

Well-established and profitable companies will often look to use their reserves and investments, accrued from the profits of earlier years, as a source of finance to pay for expansion of new developments. For the average small business this option

151

is just a dream for the future. Start-up businesses have the problem of raising the money to start the company before they can make the profits to create the reserves.

Long-term loans from financial institutions

It is often said that it is easier for a business to borrow £10 million than £10 000. Most of the merchant banks and financial institutions have little inclination to be involved in setting up long-term loans for less than £250 000, as the time and effort involved does not justify the potential profit. This is no problem for larger organizations, but it does leave small firms very much at the behest of the high street banks. Long-term loans are invariably secured, if not by property or assets, then by stocks or shares or by a debenture. Interest and capital repayments are made monthly or quarterly, with interest rates set at prearranged levels. Arranging the loans invariably incurs legal costs, and larger loans can take several months to negotiate and set up.

Chapter 9   Sales and marketing

Chapter 9
Chapter 9

The vast majority of people who are setting out to start a new business can usually tell you about how their goods or services will be made or provided, what basic resources are needed and roughly what each item will cost, but their most common deficiency is a lack of marketing knowledge and sales skills. Unless they have worked in a marketing environment, they will often not know how to research their market and how to prepare a marketing plan. Similarly, without having worked in a sales capacity they are likely to be unaware of the skills needed to identify potential customers, to investigate and match their needs and to close the sale. In fact there are many who do not even realize that sales and marketing are two fundamentally different disciplines. Marketing is concerned with identifying the level of demand for the goods or services, where potential customers might be found, the competition which exists, and creating a mixture of product features and means of delivery that will ensure the goods or services will be desirable. Sales is about actually persuading the customer to buy the goods, to pay the right price for them and then to come back to you for more at a later date. It is quite possible to make excellent goods for which there is a potentially high demand in a ready-made market, but without the sales skills to actually make the customer buy them they will just sit on the shelves.

The objective of this chapter is, first, to describe the processes of market research, identifying suitable market segments, and then designing a marketing plan. Second, we will examine some basic sales skills and techniques that should assist the reader, and show how these can be implemented to meet the objectives of the marketing plan.

For the NVQ Level 3 Business Planning students, the chapter corresponds with Unit A5, 'Develop a strategy for marketing and sales', which is concerned with market research, preparing marketing and sales plans, and in identifying ways in which the effectiveness of these can be assessed. In that respect it follows the same four stages described above.

Stokes (1998: 239–44) describes small business marketing as something of a paradox. On the one hand small firms regard marketing as being an activity for larger organizations, and yet their very flexibility and responsiveness to customer needs is the epitome of good marketing practice. Certainly by the very nature of their limited size, turnover and profit, small firms are much less able to commit such large percentages of their gross profit to marketing activities as their larger counterparts. Many owner-managers lack marketing skills, apart from those they may have picked up empirically and, then, often through making mistakes along the way, or as a result of following 'gut instinct'. Others do not go beyond basic essential sales activities, having to focus on day-to-day survival, with little time or inclination for long-term strategic planning. So, what are they missing?

Market research

Market research is an ongoing process that seeks the answers to a range of questions in the ever changing market environment:

- How large is the market for my goods or services?

- Is the market growing, static or shrinking?

- What proportion of the market do I command?

- What potential proportion could I achieve?

- What would I need to do to achieve that?

- Are there any barriers to entering the market or to expanding within it?

- What resources will I need, and over what timescale?

- What problems can I anticipate?

- Is the effort worthwhile, or should I consider an alternative?

- Who are my competitors and what are they offering?

- Are their goods or services as good as mine?

- What are the key features my customers are looking for, and can I meet these?

- What are the prevailing prices, and can I meet or beat these and make a profit?

It seems hardly surprising when faced with this package of questions that many owner-managers decide to take the simplest option of reacting to demand rather than forecasting and planning ahead to meet it. Unfortunately, little research has been carried out into the relative survival and growth rates of those who do employ market research techniques as part of their business planning, compared with the numbers of those who do not. Nevertheless, simple common sense tells us that the more we know about our customers and our markets, then the more chance there is of maximizing opportunities and minimizing risks, which has got to improve the chances of survival and growth of any business.

If we summarize the main aspects which are covered by the range of questions above, we are looking at four main areas: the size and nature of the market itself, the proportion which we hope to gain, our competitors and their offerings, and the prospects for our own goods or services within the market. We need to examine these in more detail.

The size and nature of the market

The first question we must consider is the scale of the market. Is it an international market or part of one, such as the oil or motor vehicle industries? There may be little hope of competing directly with Ford or Toyota, but there still may be an opportunity to supply them with specialist components. Is it a national industry like the market for Cheddar cheese or English sausages? Here there may be a good chance of overcoming any barriers to entry, such as high levels of competition, by targeting a special niche in the market. Is it a local market, such as a therapeutic service provided within a small geographical area? Here you would need to be even more aware of the importance of identifying and targeting the needs of the customer, rather than simply promoting the quality of the product or the service.

There is usually plenty of research data and findings about specific markets, available at international and national levels, through trade journals and associations, economic reports and analyses, national and regional statistics, etc. Not only can the overall size and growth potential of the market be established, but the respective share of key players can usually be realistically estimated by someone who knows the market well. The NVQ performance criteria for Element A5.1 require the use of valid and reliable information from published sources. However, at local level it is much harder to find the necessary direct information, and even at regional level the information may be aggregated with that of other markets within economic development reports, rendering it too general to be of much use to a new small firm. If, therefore, the published sources are inadequate or irrelevant, this should be pointed out within the business plan, along with details of alternative sources used and the reasons why these are suitable.

The target market share

If the level of supply within the particular market has not reached full capacity, then the target market share may well be determined by the capacity to produce and supply for that market. But if there is already a good deal of competition within it, then the target may need to be more modest as, without heavy investment, it may prove hard to break into a new market let alone subsequently to sustain and expand market share. Almost certainly the competitors will have something to say about a new entrant to the market and may vigorously compete to keep the newcomer out. Actually determining the target market share usually requires some specialist knowledge of the market sector to ensure that the targets are reasonable and realistic. It also implies some knowledge of the type of sales and promotional activities that would be required in order to penetrate the market to the required extent.

The nature of the competition

At international and national level the key players within an industry or service sector are usually well known to each other, and in many areas have regular contact with each other on matters of mutual interest (e.g. credit control, lobbying against new legislation etc.). Where formal links do not exist at company level between rival organizations, there are still nearly always informal links existing at a personal level. These may be between former work colleagues who have changed companies, or who may have trained together in the past, or who may even have met at trade exhibitions or conferences. Having worked in the licensed trade, computing and horticultural industries, I can vouch for the fact that even the most serious business rivalry usually breaks down after a few drinks. What is important is the amount of business that is transacted via informal contacts, and the marketing knowledge that can be gleaned and shared.

Where goods and services are concerned, anyone who is not a total newcomer to the market will normally have a good idea of who the competitors are and what they have to offer. More detailed technical information or price lists can usually be obtained by telephone request or by posing as a potential customer. Do not feel guilty or apprehensive about this approach, it happens all of the time and sooner or later someone will do it to you. Other information can be obtained from local trade directories, *Yellow Pages, Thomson Local* etc., and very often your own bank manager or Local Enterprise Agency may be able to help. Remember though, you are not just interested in finding out who your competitors are, but what goods or services they offer, at what price and with what unique or special selling features.

Comparing your own goods or services

Having examined the competition and their offerings, you now need to turn to your own goods and services to determine how they match up both to the competitors and to the nature of demand within the market as a whole. Is the price right or is it too high or too low? If I pitch my prices lower than those of my competitors, will I sell more? Is the quality right? Should I sell my products on the basis of quality rather than price? Does the market want a solid but cheap belt-and-braces product, or would a more refined and expensive alternative sell better? Perhaps there is a place for both types of product amongst different customers.

Another aspect of market research into goods or services is that of product testing, wherein the products are test marketed to establish consumer reactions and response. Depending on the product this may also have to involve some advertising or promotion as might be expected to accompany a product launch. A good example of this is the consumer testing of specific goods in discrete television franchise areas before they are launched on a national basis. Other products or services may be tested by market research surveys in supermarkets, town centres or door to door, where quality can be evaluated against price bands, using questions about how much people would be prepared to pay for the product, and their reactions to the presentation and packaging, etc.

At this point we also need to examine the relative costs and profitability. Which products will provide you with the best contribution to your overheads and profit? What proportion of less profitable goods or services can you afford to sell without adversely affecting your chances of survival? In Chapter 6 under 'The break-even analysis', we looked at an example where a higher sales volume at a slightly lower level of contribution caused a drop in overall sales revenue and subsequent profit. This is where it is important to link the marketing aspects of the business to the financial planning process, as they are essentially interdependent. The expectancy from this part of your market research is that it will help you to decide the position of your goods or services in the marketplace, and your pricing policy for them. Invariably you may find that you have a combination of products or prices appropriate to different sectors of the marketplace. This leads us conveniently into the next section which is concerned with the different segments which occur within an overall market.

Market segmentation

Market segmentation is best described as the process of analysing the demand for particular goods or services, breaking them down into distinctive segments and then identifying the characteristics of each segment to produce a marketing plan for that particular segment. In more simple terms, we are trying to identify the various groups or types of customers that share similar patterns of demand, to which we will be attempting to sell our goods or services, and then to target our sales effort towards those groups. This process is most easily illustrated by the following case study.

> Ivor Mop is in the process of setting up a contract cleaning business. He has identified four basic types of client who will provide the bulk of his business (Figure 9.1) and the specific characteristics of these clients in terms of their types of service, quality and price motivation, relative profit margins and percentages of the total expected business. As a result of this process he has established a combination of client-types which give him a balanced combination of regular high-value but low-profit contracts as his 'bread and butter' business, tempered with less regular but very profitable special work. His marketing plan can be set up to target the needs of each of these four segments. He knows that for large local authorities and school contracts he must be competitive on price whilst meeting prescribed standards of cleanliness. For office-based private companies price is still relevant, but reliability and quality of service are most important. Private individuals are willing to pay more for quality service coupled with flexibility, but they still expect value for money. Special deep-clean contracts are the most profitable, often resulting from pressure by local environmental health officers (EHOs), needing rapid response at inconvenient times. It would be hard to concentrate on this type of work as the core business because it is not sufficiently regular, but when it does arise it makes a very healthy contribution to profit margins and complements the less profitable but more regular core business that forms the bulk of Ivor's sales turnover.

Case Study

The process of identifying market segments allows you to select those that are worthy of the most effort and investment, based on the potential returns that they offer. Each segment will require a different approach in terms of the marketing mix, as described in the case study. Segmentation can be based on a

Type of Organization	Examples	Contract value Per annum	Profit margin	Service criteria	Financial or Quality motivation	Service requirements	Percentage of total business
Public sector, large	Govt. depts, schools, local authorities	£200k–£500k	10%–20%	On-going reliability	Cost motivated within specified standards	Regular full time and part time staff	30%
Private companies	Office based service and high-tech companies	£100k	15%–25%	On-going reliability, and often security sensitive	Quality service at reasonable price	Regular morning or evening	50%
Private individuals	Owners of large private homes	£10k–£15k	30%	Regular service with flexibility when needed. Honest staff	Quality service but value for money	Daily cleaning with periodical special work e.g. pool cleaning	15%
Hotel and catering trade	Hotels and restaurants	£3k–£5k	75%	Available at short notice, and anti-social hours	Rapid efficient high quality service, with minimal disruption	Annual and special 'deep cleans' to kitchens for EHO visits	5%

Figure 9.1 Market segmentation example

number of differing factors including customer needs, location, potential contribution or profit, age, sex or social status, buying habits, or simple points of common interest. These can be prioritized in various ways, in terms of the number of customers in each segment, the relative profitability of each segment, their location or accessibility or the amount of time and investment required to generate business. Once the factors have been prioritized, we can then start to formulate our marketing mixes to target the individual segments, to address those priorities.

The marketing plan for any product or service is concerned with formulating the right mixture of characteristics of the product and the way in which it is supplied and presented, so as to maximize its value and interest to the target groups of customers which have been identified within the market research process. To explain this more simply, let us take the Ivor Mop case study from the previous section. Ivor has identified catering kitchens as a potential market segment for his services. His marketing mix for that service will involve specifying the type of service (deep-cleaning of kitchens in preparation for, or in response to, environmental health inspections), the way in which it is delivered (response at short notice, working overnight and at weekends) and the key selling points (minimum disruption to working activities), which justify the premium price and high profit margin. His promotional activities will involve the direct targeting of customers by trade journal adverts, mail shots and by sales appointments with local potential clients, and the EHOs who inspect them.

The marketing plan

Traditional marketing theory expounds the four key elements of the marketing mix as being Product, Price, Promotion and Place, although it has been argued (Broome and Bitner, 1981) that for service industries People, Process and Physical aspects should also be considered. The idea is that for each product or service being offered, there is an appropriate combination of these factors that will optimize the sales potential to the respective market segments. Where a product or service is relevant to more than one segment, then the components of the marketing mix will be modified accordingly to match the needs of the respective segments. In reality, it is a common-sense problem-solving process applied to the needs of marketing, the value of which is acknowledged by the fact that it has been in use without challenge or major modification, for many years.

Product

The product element of the marketing mix is essentially concerned with the customers' perceptions and expectations of the goods or services, and covers a broad variety of aspects. There is the basic quality of the product, its durability and whether or not it will be fit for the purpose for which it was acquired. Linked to this are the aspects of warranty and after sales service in the event of there being faults or problems with the quality. The product may be of a very satisfactory or high quality, but there is also the question of its perception by the customer as giving value for money, i.e. does the quality correspond to the cost. If the quality is seen as being low compared with the cost, it will constitute poor value for money; but if it is perceived as being high in relation to cost, it will be good value for money. This aspect becomes particularly significant at times when money is tight, at the lower or utility end of the market, and when there is an abundance of competitors' products around. Also related to value for money are the range of applications or uses of the product, i.e. the uniqueness or relative usefulness of the goods or services. A good illustration of this is the range of gadgets or extras that is offered with goods such as food processors and electric drills to make them appear more versatile than competitors' tools.

The product part of the marketing mix is not just concerned with the quality and utility of the goods or services; it must also consider aspects of style and appearance as perceived by the potential customer. In particular the packaging and presentation, the brand name and the image it creates, and again the uniqueness of the product. This is especially true in premium markets where the image and uniqueness, often coupled with restricted outlets or supply, can attract status value to the product, with commensurately higher prices and profit margins. This is precisely why you cannot buy Versace clothes in the local Co-op or Gucci handbags in Woolworths.

Price

In practical terms, price is concerned with finding out how much we can charge for the goods or services to maximize profit margins without reducing the level of sales volume. Again this is a matter of customer perception, as we need to consider the price level in terms of value for money, and the price level in terms of competitors' products and prices. We may be able to charge a higher price than our competitors if the customers perceive the quality and value for money of our products to be substantially better than the competition. But the lower the differential between the products, then the lower the price difference must be. We may in fact choose to undercut the competition to buy market share through increased sales. However, such a move can also adversely affect sales, in that a substantially lower price may encourage the customers to infer that the products are in some way inferior to those supplied by competitors.

When formulating the pricing policy of the product we must also consider aspects of discounts, credit terms and payment terms, particularly if we are distributing via a wholesale and/or retailer network. If favourable, the terms and discounts can act as substantial incentives to stock or promote our products. Conversely, if poor, the terms and discounts may be a disincentive to sell the product, or result in the vendor selling it at an unfavourable price compared with competitors' goods. After all, the wholesalers and retailers are as much concerned with their profit margins as we are with our own.

Place

The place aspect of the marketing mix is not just concerned with establishing where the customers can obtain the goods or services. It is important to define the geographical areas in which the business will operate and, within those areas, outlets and their locations can be specified. Place is also about establishing and defining distribution channels, e.g. via wholesaler or retailer networks, by direct supply and delivery, by mail order etc. The choice of distribution channels will also have implications for the availability of the products, in terms of transport and supply lines, stock levels and inventories etc., which raises a number of further questions. Will you be supplying retailers through regular weekly deliveries, enabling them to hold relatively low stocks, or perhaps monthly where stock-holding will need to be higher, with consequential implications for the payment terms of your distributors? Will you choose to operate on a reduced profit margin to enable you to use wholesalers who will hold regional stocks for the retailers, thus reducing your own distribution costs? Will you be allocating exclusive sales areas to your distributors, or will they be competing against each other?

Promotion

Promotion encompasses the whole range of sales and advertising activities that could be employed. You may decide to employ a sales force to carry out direct personal selling to your potential customers. Alternatively, this work could be carried out by sales agents, or by sales staff employed by your distributors. The latter may be cheaper for you, but will it be as effective, as those same sales people may also be selling competitors' products.

The promotion part of the marketing mix also involves identifying the appropriate forms of advertising your goods or services, whether it be through national television, local radio, newspapers and magazines, specialist trade journals, mail shots, advertising hoardings, tethered balloons, *Yellow Pages*, exhibitions, trade fairs, county shows, telesales calls, sealed tenders for contracts or a stall in the local market. Not only must you identify the most suitable forms of advertising, you must also select those which are the most affordable and which are likely to give you the best return on your investment. Word of mouth recommendation is a very cheap and superb form of promotion, but it is both slow and outside your control, and so cannot be relied upon to produce results. In contrast, trade fairs and exhibitions are expensive and time-consuming, but if chosen carefully, they can offer a captive audience with a potentially high level of interest in your products, and a good chance of achieving immediate orders.

Another aspect linked to advertising is the use of special offers or sales promotions to generate interest in your products and to persuade potential customers to try them. We see this used frequently in supermarkets where new products are launched on the basis of 'buy one and get one free' bargains, or tasting sessions for food items accompanied by money-off vouchers. Obviously, these methods are not appropriate to every form of goods or services, so the promotional activity must be designed to match the product. Beauty and therapy treatments are often offered on a 'five for the cost of four treatments' basis. Gyms and fitness clubs offer discounts for annual membership to encourage regular patronage, magazines offer discounts for prepaid subscriptions, etc. Breweries offer publicans large discounts for bulk purchases in advance of the busy Christmas period, to ease delivery problems. Effective promotion is all about finding out what appeals to your particular customers and then using a little imagination to trigger their interest in your product.

People

Where services as opposed to physical goods are being supplied, then people become a more important element, particularly in terms of the image that they project to the prospective customers. This is not just a question of the impressions created by dress or physical appearance; it applies to knowledge and behavioural aspects of the interaction with customers. We are talking about technical knowledge of products and services which can create (or, if absent, can destroy) customer confidence. It is also about the attitude shown to customers in terms of behaviour, e.g. friendliness of reception staff, helpfulness of sales staff, a positive interest shown in solving customer problems, etc., and in building long-term customer–client relationships, which together reflect the overall culture of the business.

Physical

The physical aspects include the sales environment and, in particular, the impression created by the parts of the premises seen by the customers. Is the reception area clean and tidy, and tastefully decorated, or are the furnishings tatty and the space cluttered? Does the organization project an image of being well organized and professional? If you are in doubt about your premises, ask yourself the question, 'How would I feel about walking into this environment if it belonged to one of my suppliers? Would I feel comfortable, embarrassed or downright disgusted?'

Process

The process part of the marketing mix is related to the general provision of quality products and customer service. It involves ensuring that company policies and procedures are conducive to meeting the customers' needs and to providing smooth provision of service to consistent standards. It can relate, for example, to the discretion given to employees to apply flexibility or to modify procedures in order to assist customers, or it can relate to involving customers in product development, or in seeking ways to improve the standards of service.

Sales activities

The promotion section of the marketing mix should provide the basic structure for determining the methods of sales activity which will be employed according to which are the most appropriate for reaching the customer target groups. Typically this would include a combination of several of the following:

The sales plan

- *Cold-calling by telephone.* This is basically a numbers game, with large numbers of contacts, at relatively low unit cost, but usually resulting in quite a low rate of positive interest or response, even when the targeted calls have been carefully selected. The normal approach is to try to identify categories of businesses that might possibly be interested in the product (often from *Yellow Pages* or *Thomson Local*), and then to make telephone contact to find the appropriate person or decision-maker within those organizations. In recent years the double glazing industry has given this type of sales activity a bad name and, of course, the results largely depend on the skills of the individuals who are making the calls being both competent at doing the job and being able to talk convincingly about the product if they get through to the right person. To achieve positive indications of interest from 5–10 per cent of those called upon would generally be regarded as very good, and typically to convert 10 per cent of those into an actual sale would also be very good.

- *Mail shots*, like cold telephone calls, have seriously declined in value in recent years, simply due to the sheer proliferation of junk mail that falls through our letterboxes just about every day of the year. Personally speaking, I just throw circulars and all junk mail straight in the bin with no more than a cursory glance, and any obvious circular remains unopened in the envelope. Circulars containing personalized letters are read to the bottom of the first paragraph at least (unless they bear insurance company logos) to determine any relevance or usefulness, before being discarded. Sadly though, the amount of money uselessly wasted every day on postage and printing is vast, and all too often occurs because business owners are too lazy to take a more proactive attitude towards other methods of sales or promotion.

- *Cold-call visits* are much more time-consuming and costly, and therefore need to be carefully planned to avoid wasted effort by calling on the wrong type of customer. They also need to be well organized to minimize the cost of travelling between calls and to optimize the use of the sales person's time. For this reason a good sales person will often use calls for information gathering, for future reference. For example, Mr Dai Appy is a salesman employed to sell farming products in rural Wales, where distances between customers are long. If he has two positive sales appointments in a particular area, then he will use the rest of the day to make a number of cold calls on other local farmers. This serves three purposes by maintaining the profile of his company through regular contact, seeking information about future possible needs which will lead to subsequent sales, and making new contacts which can be followed up at a later date. Cold-calling, then, is more of a longer-term sales activity best used to complement other sales effort. It is not the easiest thing to do, and takes time and practice and quite a bit of nerve to do well, which is why many people dislike doing it. However, as a long-term process it can produce positive results.

- *Planned sales activity* involves a combination of the previous methods, and constitutes a much more professional approach, resulting in better use of time and a higher proportion of positive results. For example, a cold telephone call might be used to do no more than find the name of the key person or decision-maker in an organization. This is followed by a short and concise personal letter of no more than one page which outlines the products or services offered, and tells the key person that they will be contacted within a few days to request an appointment for the sales person to meet them. After that it is down to the skill of the sales person and the quality of goods or services on offer.

- *National or regional television or local radio advertising* is relatively expensive but does guarantee coverage of a wider audience. National television is excellent for consumer products, but highly expensive. Local radio stations are cheaper, but with less coverage, although they always seem to do quite well in promoting regional events.

- *The national press* is again expensive and often too broad to be of value to many businesses, although the travel industry seems to find it productive. Local papers are good for local products and particularly local services, and are more reasonably priced. Most specialist products or services are advertised in trade journals or magazines where the cost is justified by the readership which will have been identified as a potential customer group.

Sales skills

For a new or aspiring owner-manager with no previous sales experience the most daunting prospect is that of having to sell their goods or services. Selling is a skill that has to be learnt and practised if it is to achieve good results on a regular basis. The biggest mistake that most new sales people make is to try to push and sell the range of products in their portfolio, whereas someone with more experience will listen carefully to clients, and probe to identify their specific problems and needs. Only then are the products revealed, and in such a way that they offer potential solutions to the customer's needs. A Dexion salesman once told me: 'I sell solutions to problems, not storage and materials handling systems.' It is important to sell on quality and benefits rather than on lowest price. If nothing else, there is then still scope to negotiate on price at a later stage, but if a competitor beats you on both price and quality, you are out of the running.

It is also important to be open and honest with the client, to retain both credibility and the opportunity of returning at a later date. Do not promise what you cannot deliver, and do not be afraid to say if you cannot meet the client's requirements on this occasion. Buyers are as much professionals as sales people, and they not only appreciate an honest answer which saves their valuable time, but they will usually be receptive to a later approach when your product might be the real answer to their problem.

Many people who are new to sales find it hard or embarrassing to close the deal, or to actually ask the client for an order. In fact some buyers will make a point of waiting to be asked before committing themselves, particularly with young or new sales people. If you are uncomfortable about asking outright 'Can I take your order today?', then try 'When can I expect to receive your order?' or 'When would you like us to deliver?' Another approach is to ask the question 'Can you see any reason why our products will not meet your needs?' If a reason is given then you have an open opportunity to answer and overcome it. If the client has no objections then you have a direct lead into ask for the order.

Finally remember that not all business is good business, so do not be afraid to walk away from a contract or a sale if you are not happy about the terms of trade or your potential profit margins. You deserve to make a reasonable profit just as much as do the people to whom you are selling, and most professional buyers appreciate this fact. The sale should be treated as a potential starting point for a longer-term customer–supplier relationship, and as such needs to be established on equitable terms, so do not sell yourself or your business short.

The sales plan is about defining the range and combination of promotional activities that will be employed to persuade customers to buy the products. The hardest part however, is actually setting targets for sales volumes and revenues. If the market research has been done properly, then there should be some positive indications as to the overall size of the market and the potential volume that can be achieved within that market. The next problem is to try and identify how much of that potential volume could realistically be achieved. This may be influenced not just by sales capacity, but by restrictions imposed by the capacity of production and/or distribution facilities, or the time available for the provision of a service. For example, a consultancy firm employing three staff may be able to offer up to 120 hours of service per month per member of staff, an overall total of 4320 hours per annum, but it could not meet a contract requiring 2500 hours of work in just a three month period.

Setting targets and measuring achievement

Element A5.4 of the NVQ Level 3 Business Planning is concerned with specifying how the success of the marketing and sales plans will be assessed, and there are a number of ways in which this can be achieved, providing some very useful and usable results and information:

- In preparing the budgetary plan for the business, certain sales volumes will have to have been identified and formulated. These in effect constitute targets against which actual performance can be monitored on a month by month basis.

- The budgetary plan itself constitutes a summary of sales revenue targets which, again, can be monitored on a monthly basis.

- The budget will also include forecasts of expenditure for advertising and promotion. How does the actual expenditure compare with those forecasts? When expenditure has occurred, has it resulted in the expected increases in sales that it was designed to generate?

- What sort of response rates are you receiving from sales activities, e.g. in terms of the numbers of enquiries generated by each advertisement and the numbers of those that were converted in actual sales. Similarly, you can measure the response rates and achievement rates for cold telephone calls, cold sales calls, planned sales visits, mail shots, etc. If you had actually set targets for these beforehand you may well want to compare the targets and the outcomes, probably using the results to set more realistic targets for the coming year. If not, then you will now have the data to enable you to set targets for the future.

- From your expenditure figures, you can calculate the relative costs of different sales activities, cold calls, telesales, mail shots and various forms of advertising. The figures showing response rates and rates of conversion into sales can then be applied to these various activities to identify, for example, the cost per enquiry for each advertisement or the cost of each sale resulting from cold calling.

- Finally, the relative costs of the various sales activities can be compared with the revenues generated, to determine the most cost-effective methods, which will then feed into your marketing and sales plans for the forthcoming year.

References

Broome, B. H. and Bitner, M. J. (1981). *Marketing Strategies and Organizational Structures for Service Firms*. In Donnolly, J. and George, W. R. (eds). *Marketing of Services*. American Marketing Association.

Stokes, D. (1998). *Small Business Management: A Case Study Approach*. Letts.

Further reading

Institute of Management (1995). *Preparing a Marketing Plan*. IoM.

Lancaster, G. and Reynolds, P. (1995). *Marketing*. IoM and Butterworth-Heinemann.

Macdonald, M. H. B. (1995). *Marketing Plans: How to Prepare Them and How to Use Them*. Butterworth-Heinemann.

Robinson, T. (1999). *You and your Business: Marketing*. SFEDI.

Sowter, C. V. (1995). *Marketing for the Non-Marketing Manager*. McGraw Hill.

Chapter 10 Monitoring
Chapter 10
Chapter 10
and controlling quality

In Chapter 7 we examined some of the financial monitoring and control systems which are suitable for use by a small business. In this chapter we are concerned with the non-financial systems, which essentially fall under the heading of quality management. This involves defining quality standards, examining the ways in which we build quality systems into our products and services, and identifying the methods that are suitable to monitor and control the effectiveness of those quality systems.

The objective of this chapter is to assist the reader to:

- identify the aspects of the business that are critical to the provision of quality goods and services;

- establish realistic quality standards for the business which are relevant to the aims and objectives of the business;

- set up monitoring and control procedures which will enable those standards to be achieved on a consistent basis.

For the NVQ candidate, this chapter links to Unit A.6 of the NVQ Level 3 Business Planning qualification, 'Investigate ways to ensure that the business operates to quality standards'. This requires the candidate to demonstrate a knowledge and understanding of quality management, and competence in applying that knowledge within a small business. In order to satisfy the evidence requirements of this unit, the candidate must demonstrate that they have considered the impact of quality on the way the business operates, that they understand how to utilize quality procedures to meet business objectives, and that they can define targets and quality standards, and the criteria for assessing the achievement of those standards.

The three most frequently used quality procedures against which businesses can be assessed for accreditation are the ISO 9000 standards for quality systems and procedures (formerly BS 5750), the ISO 14001 standards which relate to environmental quality, and the Investors in People (IIP) award for organizations which meet specified standards in staff training and development, personnel systems, equal opportunities, and other people-related quality systems. The important common feature of these is that they are not just a one-off process. Once awarded, the standards of accreditation have to be maintained, and the organization is subject to periodic inspections by independent assessors whom it must satisfy in order to retain the accreditation. The assessment criteria are rigorous and comprehensive, and unless the standards are maintained on a consistent basis, the organization can have its ISO or IIP approval suspended or withdrawn.

Why does a business need to bother with Investors in People or ISO 9000?

For many businesses the desire to achieve ISO 9000 or IIP accreditation is not always altruistic, as possession of one or other of these is becoming an increasing requirement for inclusion on lists of preferred suppliers, or for competitive tenders. In the case of some major organizations that are themselves accredited, they simply refuse to buy from any suppliers who are not already accredited or working towards accreditation. At first glance, this approach may seem rather harsh, but it does make a good deal of sense in that a supplier's possession of a quality accreditation should ensure that goods or services obtained from that supplier will be of the right quality. The

International Standards Organization (ISO) standards, which superseded the British Standard, are accepted on a European-wide basis, so possession of one of these is particularly important for firms trading in international markets. The implementation of quality systems can also bring about a range of further direct benefits including:

- Reduced customer complaints and returned or rejected goods. In addition to the obvious cost savings of not having to process complaints or handle returned goods and replace them, in the longer term the enhanced reputation of quality goods or services will increase sales.

- Customer retention is improved leading to a reduction in selling costs, as less sales effort goes into replacing lost customers. This means that the sales effort can be directed to expanding the customer base to increase turnover and profits. This is discussed in more detail in Chapter 11.

- Quality production systems work towards eliminating faults or problems by ensuring that they do not occur in the first place. This idea of Quality by Design is aimed at ensuring that all aspects of design and production are geared towards getting the product right first time and every time. In the short term this may result in an initial increase in costs, but in the longer term costs will fall, as there is no longer the need for extensive and detailed inspection. Similarly, as more goods are produced to the correct standard, the costs of rejection or reworking are also greatly reduced. For example, quality systems will discourage the purchase of components from the cheapest supplier on the basis of price alone. The cheapest supplier's components may have a failure rate of perhaps 10 per cent, which if they remain undetected could result in a failure or rejection rate in the finished article of 10 per cent or more. However, for a small increment in the cost of the components, the failure rate might be reduced to 1 or 2 per cent resulting in huge savings on reworking, repairs or replacement and, of course, savings resulting from the reduced amount of waste materials generated.

- The use of quality circles and an ethos of continuous improvement amongst staff tends to result in problems being noticed before they develop. Staff become more positive about their roles and duties, as the quality process encourages ownership or responsibility. Planned training and development programmes for staff also enable them to become more efficient at their work as they gain more detailed knowledge of the processes. Staff involvement in regular quality meetings in work time (quality circles) where supervisors have the same status as ordinary staff, promotes a coherent approach in working towards the achievement of quality systems of work and quality standards.

- Regular internal audits, and periodic external assessments or inspections ensure that quality standards are maintained on an ongoing basis. Initially this may be a matter of fear of outside criticism, but as time goes on, it usually develops into a matter of pride in the organizational systems.

- Management and communication systems and procedures are improved which allows for better planning, and easier decision-making and problem-solving. In particular, the improved communications between levels of staff tends to promote earlier warnings of possible problems. It is the difference between shooting the messenger who is the bearer of bad news, and praising the same person for being astute enough to spot a potential difficulty, which demonstrates a basic shift in organizational culture from punishment by blame to motivation by praise.

In the first half of the century great emphasis was placed on quality control in manufacturing and production environments.

How does the process work?

This was based on the idea of ensuring that customers received quality products by inspecting them at each stage of the production process and rejecting any faulty or substandard items. Perversely, high (and costly) rates of rejection were often regarded as a sign of good quality products, as only the best were allowed to pass. Naturally, the more thorough and rigorous the inspection, the more costly the process became. Following on from quality control came the idea of quality assurance, where operations management systems were employed to make production processes more efficient, and to eliminate faults in the production process. This was perhaps a move in the right direction but it still did not tackle problems which were inherent within products and systems by virtue of the way in which they had been designed.

The Total Quality Management (TQM) approach has been around since the post-war period, and the American TQM guru W. Edwards Deming, started to employ its principles in the re-establishment of post-war Japan, the Americans having failed to take it on board despite Deming's efforts to persuade them. Then TQM started to grow in popularity in the USA and Europe in the 1970s. It focused initially on the marketing principle of identifying the customer's needs, both the customers in the marketplace and those internal customers in the production chain within the organization. Once the customer need is identified, TQM works on the basis of designing standards of excellence within that product, and then designing quality systems in the organization which would ensure that the excellence of the product can be achieved and delivered to the customer on a regular and consistent basis – hence the phrase 'getting it right first time and every time'.

How do we go about achieving it?

In larger organizations the usual route is to either employ a firm of quality management consultants to examine all of the various systems used by the organization, or to appoint a trained quality services manager to carry out the same process,

179

to design the standards to which the organization will work, to produce the manuals and procedures, and to seek and subsequently maintain accreditation. Overall this can be a long and very expensive exercise which is likely to be well beyond the resources of most small businesses, especially those just starting up. If accreditation is essential, then some expenditure must be expected, although advice, and sometimes financial assistance, can be obtained from local councils, Local Enterprise Agencies, Business Links, etc. If however, you just wish to design and build quality systems into your business without gaining formal accreditation, then the process can be simplified, although not to the extent that you can start cutting corners – that is not what quality management is about.

For someone starting up in business, probably the easiest way to go about formulating a quality management policy is to start by looking at all the systems and procedures that operate within the business, both now and in the foreseeable future; and having listed these, for every one of them ask yourself 'What can conceivably go wrong?' A good starting point might be to look at what happens when a customers enquire about your products or services, and then to follow the sequence through, from receipt of order, production, delivery, invoicing, after sales service, etc. – and, of course, do not forget the administrative processes which support each of these stages. We will take a hypothetical example of a plumber, Mr Mick Sturbs, who is a sole trader employing a young lad to assist him, and we will work through the various stages of handling a customer enquiry and carrying out the work:

1   Mick has a weekly advertisement in the local paper, which generates most of his business. What can go wrong? Does he pay the paper promptly and regularly to ensure continuity of advertising? Is the advertisement clear about the types of service he provides and about how to contact him? Does it project a professional image? Does it produce results in the form of enquiries for work?

2   A customer sees the advert and enquires about his services. Does the customer find it easy to contact him? Does someone take messages for him while he is out? Are they positive, helpful and competent in answering, or do they appear rude, indifferent or disinterested? Are they knowledgeable about the business? Will they know how to contact him in an emergency? If Mick uses an answerphone, does he check it regularly during the day? Does he follow up enquiries by promptly returning the call, or do customers get tired of waiting and go elsewhere? Does he use a mobile phone to make contact easier? Are the mobile phone batteries charged regularly so that it is ready for use when needed? Are the details of each enquiry recorded carefully, or does he tend to lose details of customers and their telephone numbers? Does he respond to enquiries within a specified period of time, or do customers have to wait until he is ready?

3   A customer arranges an appointment for Mick to fix a new central heating boiler. Does he allow sufficient time in his diary to do the job properly or does he try to cram it in between other jobs? Does he build in contingency time in case he encounters a problem, or does he leave the job unfinished to return a few days later? Does he arrive on time at the customer's premises, or turn up halfway through the day? Is he polite and friendly, or rude or indifferent? Does his appearance create the right impression with the customer, or is he scruffy or wearing greasy overalls and muddy boots? Does he project a professional attitude, or does he give the impression of being a bodger? Does he make sure that he has all of the necessary equipment with him, or does he keep having to go back to get them? Has he ordered the materials in advance to ensure that they are available when needed? Has he given the customer a written quotation for the work and explained what is, and what is not, included in the price? Has he explained his terms of trade and the

arrangements for payment? Does he pay his own suppliers regularly and reliably to ensure that his supplies are always available? Is his assistant competent and knowledgeable, or just a gopher?

4   Mick fits the new central heating boiler for his customer. Has he used good quality materials that will ensure a lasting job, or has he cut corners to boost his profit? Has the work been completed to a professional standard, or has he bodged it because he is short of time? Has he checked any work carried out by his assistant? Has he advised the customer of any safety measures needed, and how to use the boiler properly? Has he checked that the customer understands these? Has he provided the customer with the manufacturer's warranty for the boiler? Does he offer a warranty for his own workmanship? Has he left the premises in a clean and tidy condition and removed any rubbish? Has he provided the customer with a detailed invoice, and explained any variances from the estimated cost? Did he obtain the customer's approval for any extra expenditure before it was incurred? Did he check that the customer was satisfied with the work? Did he thank the customer for payment? Did he leave the customer a business card for future reference, or in case of emergencies?

5   After the job was finished did he call the customer a few days later to check that all was going well? On completion, did he record his sales income, and the various items of expenditure in his sales and purchase accounts books or petty cash book? Was any VAT that was paid or collected, recorded correctly? Were his tools cleaned and stored, and any materials such as solder replenished ready for the next job? Were any problems with the boiler reported to the manufacturer or supplier? Did he remember to top up the petrol in his van ready for the early start the following day, or will he be arriving late yet again?

The above questions are by no means exhaustive, but a wrong answer to just about any one of them could result either in a problem arising or in the client receiving an inferior level of service. Quality systems do not have to be complex to be effective. In Mick's case, his quality systems and procedures could probably be organized using a simple job sheet that incorporates a checklist of the various items. His procedure for dealing with clients' enquiries could just involve organizing an efficient answering service and mobile phone, and setting himself simple standards for response times. For example, he could check his answering service at set times during the day, and then make a point of returning any call within, say, no more than three hours of its receipt. He could note in his diary follow-up calls to clients within a week of the work being completed. He could have standard quotation forms printed, with his terms of trade on the rear. He could set his own administrative standards and systems to maintain his accounts on a weekly basis, to pay all bills promptly on the dates due and to chase his own debtors for payment. He could also arrange vocational training for his assistant, and take a short course in customer care for himself. As a qualified plumber he could maintain his membership of the appropriate trade association, and of necessity he must maintain his Council for Registration of Gas Installers (CORGI) accreditation to operate legally.

The idea of TQM still remains very much within the domain of larger organizations, although it is gradually becoming more noticeable in smaller firms. The great thing about designing and building quality into systems and procedures for small firms is that when there are still relatively few firms employing these systems, the opportunity for developing and enhancing a reputation for quality is tremendous, and so are the potential benefits for putting the business ahead of its competitors. Many larger firms state within their mission statement, the objective of becoming a 'first-choice supplier', but there is absolutely no reason why a small firm or a sole trader cannot employ quality systems to achieve the same objective within its own local market.

Not only do small businesses lack the staff and resources which larger organizations can employ to develop and maintain quality systems, they face similar problems when it comes to monitoring their quality standards and measuring their performance. But pressure of work or lack of resources should not be used as an excuse for an owner-manager to neglect the monitoring process. As we have shown in the case of Mick the plumber above, it is perfectly possible to implement quality systems within very small and simple businesses. If the systems are capable of being established quite easily, then they are equally capable of being monitored without the need for complex computer systems, or substantial staff time.

How can a small business monitor its quality systems?

In retrospect, the most obvious indicator of potential problems or of the failure of quality systems is to look at the sales volume and revenue figures which were used in the preparation of the budgetary plan. Are the figures on target? If not, do we know why this is so? Is it due to external factors beyond our control, or something we are doing wrong within the business? Have our competitors been affected in the same way? Is it due to poor forecasting, or inadequate sales effort, or to a problem with the quality of the products or services we are offering? If it is apparently a problem of quality, then there are a number of options we can employ to isolate and identify the problem or problems within our products or systems.

The obvious starting point for any business is to examine the nature of the complaints received or goods returned in order to determine whether or not these affect the whole range of products, or a specific group of them. If the complaints have been received across a whole range of goods or services, then it is probable that the source of the problem will lie within the systems used by the business. In this case it will be necessary to examine the complaints more closely, perhaps by contacting former customers who have complained, in order to seek out any common points or issues which might pinpoint the problem. If the owner of the business has proper quality systems in place, these types of common issues should already be being picked up as part of the ongoing review of quality standards. If that is not the case, then there is clearly more than one flaw in the system, which must be addressed.

If however, the complaints have been focused on a single product or product group, then it is more likely that the problem will lie within the product itself rather than the systems which deliver them, and it should be a fairly straightforward process to isolate the problem. In the case of physical goods it may be a specific component or assembly process which is the continuing source of the problem, and which can be identified as a common element amongst returned goods. If we know that the problem started at a specific time, it may be traceable to change of supplier or a variation in the assembly process. If ongoing, but gradually increasing, it may be due to a problem of wear and tear or deterioration of production machinery which, when discovered, can be rectified.

Another indication of problems are the changes in levels of customer retention, although the monitoring of these is really only applicable to businesses which supply customers on a regular basis, as opposed to one-off sales. There is always a certain amount of 'natural wastage' or turnover with customers, and over a period of time this can be established, but when these rates start to increase, it is usually indicative of either a decline in the quality problem within the products or services, or an indication that they are not up to the same standards being provided by competitors. Once again, the monitoring of these is more of a long-term process, as short-term fluctuations in customer activity tend to distort the short-term picture.

Analysing changes in sales volumes and revenues and customer retention levels, and monitoring volumes and patterns of complaints after the event is very much a reactive process, which by definition is not what quality management is all about. A more proactive approach is to monitor sales and customer responses on an ongoing basis, and this should be an inherent part of the quality systems of any business. One option is to establish a positive procedure for customer care (see Chapter 11), which will provide a prompt and efficient means of responding to and rectifying customer problems. Another way is to use customer feedback, either verbal or obtained by questionnaire, to monitor the customers' perceptions of the quality of the goods and services that you are providing. Again, the quality approach relies on prompt response and positive action to rectify any problems identified by the feedback.

Summary

- Oakland (1993) states that 'quality begins with marketing'. In the first instance we must establish the customers' needs for the goods or services we aim to provide.

- We must establish the customers' expectations of the products and services, and of the businesses that aim to provide them.

- We must analyse every stage of the production or provision of the goods or services, and the systems which support that production or provision, to identify potential problem areas, and to design those products and systems to avoid the anticipated problems.

- We must set precise, accurate and realistic standards for our products and systems, which will act as targets against which we can monitor our success in providing quality products and services.

- We must ensure that all staff involved in the business are committed to the principles of providing quality products and services, and are knowledgeable about the standards required of them, and that they have received any training necessary to enable them to achieve those standards.

- We must monitor the compliance with standards on an ongoing basis, by monitoring customer feedback, complaints, product returns, etc., to ensure that any problems are promptly addressed and rectified. In the longer term, we must monitor changes in sales volumes and revenues for our products and services, and overall customer retention, to assess the impact these are having on the overall performance of the business.

- We must review all products, systems and procedures on a regular basis to ensure that quality standards are maintained, or are modified as needed, and that these are redesigned to eliminate future potential problems when required.

- Finally, we must continue to ask ourselves the question: 'If I were one of my own customers, would I really be happy with the quality of the service and products that I am receiving from this business?'

Reference

Oakland, J. (1993). *Total Quality Management: The Route to Improving Performance*. Butterworth-Heinemann.

Further reading

Bell, D., McBride, P. and Wilson G. (1998). *Managing Quality*. IoM and Butterworth-Heinemann.

MacDonald, J. (1993). *Understanding Total Quality Management in a Week*. IoM and Headway.

Munro-Faure, L. and Munro-Faure, M. (1993). *Achieving Quality Standards: A Step by Step Guide to BS5750/ISO9000*. IoM and Pitman.

Sadgrove, K. (1995). *Making TQM Work*. Kogan Page.

Tricker, R. (1997). *ISO 9000 for Small Businesses*. Butterworth-Heinemann.

Chapter 11 Customer service

Chapter 11
Chapter 11

Chapter 11 is concerned with how the needs of customers are identified and assessed, not so much in the sense of the products or the goods and services which they require, but the ways in which those products are provided, delivered and subsequently supported by the people involved in the organization. Customer service is about formulating and implementing policies and standards of behaviour and practice, which will ensure that customers' needs are identified. It is also about developing procedures that ensure customers are treated politely, fairly and positively if things go wrong.

Invariably the customer service policy will overlap and reflect the sales and marketing plans and the quality policy of the business, as it does in effect define the way in which quality standards are implemented within the sales environment. The objectives of this chapter are to examine how to identify customer needs and expectations, and to define how they will be implemented and monitored. This chapter also relates to Unit A7 of the NVQ Level 3 Business Planning qualification, entitled 'Establish a customer service policy'. This follows the same pattern of assessing customer needs, developing policies and procedures to meet those needs, and specifying how those policies will be implemented and monitored.

We have already examined the marketing context of identifying customer needs in the market research section of Chapter 9.

The service aspects of customer needs can most effectively be determined by asking customers face to face, by telephone or by written questionnaire, whether the business is meeting the full range of their needs and expectations, where there are any gaps or shortfalls and how the customers would like to see those addressed.

Apart from the details and specifications of the products themselves, in most cases when we are talking about customer needs we are, in reality, talking about customer expectations. By this we mean what the customers expect from us as suppliers, and what the customers themselves perceive to be their needs, as opposed to what we believe them to be.

What do customers expect?

- *From the business*: pleasant and suitable surroundings which are clean, welcoming, well-lit, safe and hygienic, and living up to the general image of the business and its products or services.

- *From the staff*: sufficient staff to be available. Staff to show a friendly, interested and welcoming attitude, and to be pleasant and non-threatening. Staff should also be smart in appearance, competent and knowledgeable. Customers also expect that dealing with the organization's staff should be a pleasant experience, and free of problems, antagonism or excuses.

- *From the products, goods or services*: these should be available when wanted, fit for the purpose for which they were acquired, and at a reasonable price which constitutes value for money. User-friendly information should be provided as to where the product can be found, and about its use and operation. The product should also be supported by a friendly, helpful and efficient after sales service in the event of any problems arising.

189

First, let us differentiate between the two. Customer service is often described as the way in which we respond to customers and their problems. In contrast, customer care goes a stage further in that a customer care policy (like a TQM policy) tries to build a policy of awareness and responsiveness to the customer within the provision of the product or service as a whole, and with the intention of avoiding possible problems at a later stage. Customer care is about minimizing the occurrences that are likely to give rise to complaint, and responding quickly and positively when complaints do occur. The primary objectives of customer care are to:

Why should we bother with customer service or customer care?

- Retain customers for repeat business. The use of sales staff and advertising etc. to find new customers is an expensive process. If we can retain or at least reduce the rate of natural turnover of existing customers, then sales effort can be invested in finding extra new customers which overall will increase the sales revenues and profits of the business.

- Increase the level of trade with existing customers by improving their confidence in the business and its products or services. Dealing with the business should constitute a pleasant and problem-free experience. This again will generate extra sales revenue and profit in the longer term.

- Enhancing the reputation of the business and its quality standards. This is aimed at increasing customer loyalty and recommendation, which again adds to turnover and profit. Even customers who complain, but who are treated well in response, tend to return and to tell others about their positive experience. In contrast, poor service leads to loss of reputation and customers, and consequential reductions in turnover or the need for extra sales effort to replace lost trade

- In the longer term, the implementation of customer care policies tends to reduce the costs of operations. As in the case of quality management described in the previous chapter, by building in quality systems it is possible to reduce the need for checking and inspection, leading to a reduction in the cost of quality control. Similarly, a good customer care policy tends to reduce the occurrence of problems and to correct them before they get out of hand. Customers who do not complain often go elsewhere anyway, so the idea is to avoid complaints arising in the first place, to prevent the loss of customers. Overall the process should result in a reduction of costs as the need for inspection and remedial action is reduced.

- Within the business itself, a positive customer care policy should also have the effect of increasing job satisfaction of staff, both by the positive interaction with their customers, and by avoiding the stress and aggravation that accompany customer complaints. Once again, this should contribute to the overall efficiency of the business.

Customer expectations do not always relate to the object in question but to the potential benefits that object offers. People do not just go to restaurants for food; they go to spend a pleasant evening with friends in relaxed and convivial surroundings. Cars are not just sold on engine size, they are sold on the pleasure of driving in comfort, their reliability and economy, the exhilaration of speed and acceleration, and the image they convey. Think back to the Dexion salesman quoted in Chapter 9: 'I sell solutions to problems, not storage or materials handling systems'. Similarly, within the sales transaction and subsequent interpersonal contact, customers do not just want efficiency, they need to be made to feel important and that their custom is valued, and to have esteem and respect from the sales staff even if it is just a one-off transaction. Most important of all, the attitude projected by staff must be perceived as being genuine; no matter how obnoxious the customer, given time the positive attitude may even rub off on them. Customers are a complex mixture of personality, emotions, motivations, attitudes and needs. The more that you understand their perspectives, the better you can meet those needs.

The implication of this is that the quality ethos and customer care attitude must be an inherent part of the internal culture of the business, which implies a high level of commitment on the part of the owners, to motivate their staff and to treat them in an equitable fashion. The bottom line is that you can hardly expect your staff to treat your customers with respect and to demonstrate commitment to customer care if behind the scenes you are treating the staff like dirt. Remember, Murphy's Third Law of Universal Cock-Ups states that if you treat your staff badly they will wreak revenge through your clients, and usually at a time and place where it is guaranteed to hurt you the most. Like charity, customer care starts at home.

As we have just said, the customer care attitude must become an inherent part of the culture of the business, and the policies which are developed must work towards that end. In larger organizations this normally takes place as part of an overall TQM strategy affecting all systems and operations, and relating to the internal customers as well as those in the external marketplace. In a new business the initial primary objective is usually that of survival and growth to a level of financial stability, and only once that stability has been achieved can the proprietors move further towards enhancing growth and profit using quality systems. The fact is that irrespective of any desire to employ quality systems, most new businesses do not have the time or resources to implement these in the early stages of their existence. However, once a basic level of stability is achieved, they are in a position to move from reactive to proactive methods of working, of which the introduction of customer care policies is an obvious choice and priority.

How do we go about formu-lating a customer care policy?

Probably the most important aspect of the customer care policy is that it should coincide with, and work towards meeting, the primary objectives or mission statement of the business. In fact most businesses which actively promote policies of customer service and customer care invariably end up including reference to those policies within their objectives, particularly in service industries where the process generates the profit. The mission statement might be something like: 'The company will aim to provide a high-quality, reliable service to its clients which will establish it as a first-choice supplier in the marketplace, leading to maximization of profits and sustained and continuous growth.' The corresponding customer care statement might be something like: 'To provide a high standard of customer service and care which will enhance the reputation of the company's services leading to an expansion of its customer base and enhancing the profitability of the business.'

The policy also needs to identify how the customers of the business will be made aware of the customer care policies. Some organizations do this by incorporating their customer service standards within their printed terms of trade, although there may be a tendency for the information to be lost in the small print and therefore seldom read. Some clearly publicize their policies in their advertising material or on printed sheets which accompany receipts or sales invoices. Where physical products are produced, the information may be contained within the printed warranty or product guarantee. Others have their policies displayed prominently in their reception areas where visitors and clients can readily view them.

Most of the conventional textbooks on customer care are geared towards larger organizations, and propose commendable ideas such as creating posts of customer service manager, increasing levels of teamwork and multiskilling, integrated audio, video and data communications. These may be great for a large company, but are somewhat grandiose and impractical for the average owner-manager of a new business, who struggles to afford a secretary. What is needed then is to take some of the ideas from the big company model and to apply them on a smaller scale. So in answer to the question 'How do we go about formulating a customer care policy?' we revisit the customer expectations which we examined earlier and apply them to the small business environment. For example, we know that our customers expect to receive a positive and prompt response to enquiries. So in place of the 'integrated communications systems' of large organizations, we look at practical ways of ensuring that no call from a customer is overlooked and all enquiries receive a response within a specified period of time. In fact, within small firms the formulation of the customer care policy becomes more a case of identifying where there is a potential problem resulting from a customer expectation not being met, then finding the most practical and affordable solution for that problem, and setting basic standards for ensuring the solution is implemented.

To answer this question, let us take several examples of customer expectations that might be problematic, and offer potential solutions to these.

How do we implement the customer care policy and ensure that it is achieved?

Example 1

Problem: Customers expect someone to respond quickly to their enquiries.

Solution: If the owner-manager is not available to answer enquiries, then nominate another person to take that specific responsibility, ensuring that they have or are given basic training in telephone answering skills, and some knowledge of the products or services which you supply. Insist that all details of enquiries are logged. If no one is available, then ensure that an efficient remote-access answerphone or voicemail system is in place, preferably supported by e-mail and fax facilities.

Standards: Make regular contact with the designated staff, at least two or three times a day, to ensure that there are no outstanding queries or to provide answers to any questions which may be beyond their scope. If using answering facilities, check them at two- to three-hour intervals, log all details of enquiries and the dates and times they are received, then ensure that all messages are acknowledged immediately by telephone. Ensure that any actions arising are implemented within twenty-four hours.

Achievement: Monitor log entries to ensure that responses have been made within standard times. Check the frequency of incidents that fall outside the standards and investigate the cause of these.

Example 2

Problem: Customers expect the business premises to be clean, tidy, well lit and pleasant to be in. This can be particularly difficult for a small firm with very confined working space.

Solution: Try to divide the working part of the premises from the part accessed by customers, e.g. the reception area. Ensure that it is warm, dry, reasonably decorated, well lit, and that it is cleaned on a daily basis. Provide some basic seating to make clients comfortable and information about the firm's products or services to keep them occupied if waiting. Ensure that they are greeted and acknowledged on arrival and not kept waiting. Ensure that your staff are aware that the area must be treated differently, and reserved for clients, and why this is so.

Standards: Daily cleaning and watering of any pot plants, regular replacement of reading materials and information, e.g. weekly/monthly, periodic painting or redecoration, and replacement of damaged furniture.

Example 3

Problem: Customers expect a prompt response to problems and complaints.

Solution: Establish a procedure for handling complaints, recording details of the complainant, the nature of the problem, the customer's desired solution, etc. Allocate responsibility for handling complaints to a specific member of staff and train that person in the procedures to be followed. Establish a tracking system to ensure that complaints are followed up and resolved within specified times, and that any exceptions are flagged for action.

Standards: All complaints to be acknowledged within twenty-four hours and action taken to rectify problems within seventy-two hours of the complaint. If further time is required, the client is to be notified of the reason why and given an estimated time for resolution of the problem. Within one week of the problem being rectified, the designated person is to telephone the client to check on satisfaction, and to obtain the client's feedback on the complaints procedure, along with any outstanding problems or adverse comments. These need to be recorded and raised for discussion at the next weekly staff meeting.

The above examples have looked at just three customer expectations, the first being an example of what the customers expect from the staff of a business, the second of what is expected from the premises, and the third of what is expected of after sales service for the products. If we look back at the rest of the customer expectations described at the start of this chapter, we can see that the process used in those three examples can be extended and applied to most of the others, in some form or another, within just about any small business. The list of customer expectations are useful as a starting point for identifying ways of implementing customer care, but the owner-manager still needs to analyse the full range of other expectations which might arise from customers of his or her particular business. Each and every one of them can be treated as a potential problem area, in response to which a customer care policy will need to be formulated. Once this solution to the potential problem is proposed, and a method of implementation identified, standards can be established which will be used to define its success. The final part of the policy, then, is to identify the process and frequency with which the achievement of those standards will be monitored. That in a nutshell, is how customer care policies can be implemented in even the smallest of businesses.

Further reading

Canning, V. (1999). *Being Successful in Customer Care*. Blackhall.
Smith, I. (1997). *Meeting Customer Needs*. IoM and Butterworth-Heinemann.
Stone, M. and Young, L. (1992). *Competitive Customer Care*. Croner.

Chapter 12 Premises requirements

Chapter 12
Chapter 12

This first part of this chapter is concerned with the processes of identifying the space required for various activities, the most suitable types of premises, their locations, their relative costs and the legal aspects of acquiring premises. The second part is concerned with associated issues of insurance related to premises, but broadening out into a general overview of different types of insurances and their relevance to the owner-manager.

The objectives of Chapter 12 are to assist the potential owner manager to review his or her options in examining potential premises and to understand some of the legal implications of buying, leasing or renting commercial premises. It will also enable the reader to assess which types of insurance cover he or she should be considering for both premises, and for the business as a whole, including the physical resources considered in Chapter 13. This chapter also relates to the NVQ Level 3 Business Planning Unit A8, 'Assess the business needs for dedicated premises', which is concerned with assessing requirements, selecting suitable premises, and negotiating the terms and conditions of occupancy. Unit A8 links closely to Unit A9 'Assess the business need for physical resources' covered in Chapter 13, and it makes sense to consider the physical resource requirements before or in tandem with the premises requirements, as they tend to be interdependent. The size, volume and extent of physical resources may well predetermine the premises requirements or, conversely, the availability of premises may place limitations on the physical resources which can be utilized.

What sort of premises will I need?

Well, first, just what type of business are you running? A mobile hairdresser or are you a therapist who visits clients in their homes and who may be able to work from your own home, with just the need for a small amount of storage space. A self-employed professional consultant may also be able to do likewise by converting a spare room at home into an office; however, a small office in a commercial location might create a better image in the eyes of their clients and customers. An engineering or manufacturing process would almost certainly be looking for premises with planning consent for light industrial use, particularly if the work involved noisy machinery, dusty of dirty processes, etc. For a retail business, the location of the premises will be a primary factor as the business will need either to be in a place where the customers already go, such as a shopping mall, or in a place where it is easy and convenient for the customers to get to them, such as a retail park. A wholesaler would need to be in a central position from which customers could be supplied and, ideally, close to a good road network.

The cost of retail premises is largely determined by their location. Town centre shops are always expensive to rent, lease or buy, although because of those same high costs, many town centre shopping malls or arcades frequently have a proportion of empty property due to the high turnover rate when businesses fail, or move because of the high rents. Shops located in retail parks are also relatively expensive to rent because of the cost of providing the infrastructure – access roads and parking. In comparison, retail outlets just outside town centres and on main access routes tend to be cheaper, and those in residential areas or on the outskirts of towns can be cheaper still. The relative cost of premises on industrial or commercial estates will depend on a number of factors including their proximity to road networks and motorways, the age and condition of the premises themselves, and the extent and quality of customer parking, security and services. The same basic principle applies to storage and warehousing. To rent space in a farmer's barn may be very cheap, but remote locations and muddy access roads may not be so good in winter. On the other hand, a modern warehouse will be much more secure and accessible, but correspondingly more expensive to rent.

So, in answer to the question 'What sort of premises will I need?' we have to consider a number of factors:

- The type of business which is planned, and the type of premises most appropriate to that business. The physical environment may be important to the product or process e.g. hygienic and easy to clean for food preparation.

- Whether or not customers will need access to the premises on a regular basis, and where those customers will be coming from.

- The appearance of the premises if they will be visited by customers regularly.

- The need for easy access to motorways, road networks, rail links, airports, etc.

- The likelihood of obtaining planning consent for the proposed use.

- The need for services and facilities such as customer parking.

- The need for security.

- What the business is likely to be able to afford in the early stages.

- The space requirements.

- Convenience of access for the owner-manager.

What size premises will I need?

A good starting point for estimating this is to look at the inventory of physical resources which you will need for the business, and which is discussed in Chapter 13. Until you actually identify what fixtures and fittings, machinery, furniture, etc., you will need to run the business, and how this will need to be laid out, it is impossible to make a realistic judgement about the working area required. Probably the easiest way to start is with several large sheets of graph paper on which you can sketc.h various layouts of the 'ideal' premises. First, work out the different work areas that will be required and which need to be separated or partitioned off from each other. Let us take several examples.

Example 1

In a reasonably sized high street shop the main area will obviously be the retail section where the customers come to inspect the goods. There will also need to be a stockroom for the storage of backup stock, toilets for staff, a small office space for a desk and telephone for the manager, somewhere secure for staff to leave their bags and coats, and somewhere to make tea or coffee and to wash up. If the shop anticipates a large turnover, there may also need to be a safe within the office.

Example 2

For a small wholesaling business the main premises requirement is storage space for the products, with a small office for dealing with customer enquiries and producing invoices, etc., a toilet and wash room and small room for the delivery drivers or warehouse staff to use during breaks and in which to store their clothes. More important, however, are the dimensions of the storage area, as vertical storage of stock on pallets is far more economical and efficient than having the stock spread around the floor. The space also needs to be planned to allow access for handling equipment such as fork-lifts trucks when goods are received or dispatched, which also has implications for floor surfaces which must not be too rough, and there must be adequate door widths for access.

Example 3

A self-employed complementary therapist setting up a in practice would only need a main room in which to treat the clients, a small reception area and a toilet. The treatment room would house a desk and filing cabinet, the treatment couch, some cupboards with a work top and sink, and some screened space for clients to change behind. The space requirements here are simple and modest, but the room itself would need good heating for the comfort of clients, a washable floor, and there would need to be parking space outside for the clients' vehicles. In fact the parking area would probably need to be greater than the treatment area.

Having worked out how the space would need to be subdivided, the second stage is to ask yourself how big these areas need to be? To do this it is first necessary to work out what is going to go into each of them, and then to look at the way they will be laid out. You should allow plenty of space in which to move around, especially if stock or heavy items are to be moved using barrows, pallet trucks or fork-lift trucks. This exercise should generate a rough idea of the area needed, although real premises are invariably always the wrong shape and with power points and water supplies in the most inconvenient of places, so it pays to allow for a margin of error. There is bound to be something you have forgotten.

Another aspect which must be considered is that of growth or expansion. All too often owner-managers of new businesses fail to plan ahead and take on the smallest premises that they can manage with, just to save on short-term rental costs. As soon as the business starts to grow, those premises are outgrown, and the proprietor has to go through the expensive and time-consuming process of looking for bigger premises. Apart from the cost of moving and the disruption to trade, this can be particularly expensive if the premises are subject to a minimum rental period, where an early move might invoke a penalty clause in the rental agreement. So, you must ask yourself what size of premises might be needed to meet your planned rate of growth over the next two or three years, as the answer to this may well influence your final choice of location.

What are the options for acquiring premises?

The most appropriate way of acquiring premises is usually predetermined by the financial resources that are available within the start-up business. A lot of potential owner-managers like to start very cautiously by utilizing existing space at home, so as not to commit themselves to heavy regular expenditure on premises until they are sure that the business will take off. This is fine for some activities such as those involving the provision of services by sole traders but, for manufacturing, wholesale or retail activities, commitment to expenditure for premises is usually unavoidable. This is particularly true if the new business involves buying out another established business, such as a shop or garage, or setting up a franchised business associated with a corporate image (e.g. a MacDonalds or Wimpy outlet) where the design, décor and facilities within the premises are specified under the terms of the franchise.

The most common methods of acquiring premises are for freehold or leasehold purchase or some form of rental agreement:

Freehold ownership

Freehold ownership of premises can take two forms. In some cases the business (or its owners) will buy land and develop

203

custom-built premises. This is typically associated with well-established cash rich companies for whom the land is often a long-term capital investment. More often in small businesses, freehold premises are purchased along with the business within them (e.g. shops, pubs, off-licences), or a warehouse may be bought to house a specific business. Typically the process of freehold purchase requires the purchaser to provide 20 per cent to 25 per cent of the purchase price from their own resources, with the balance being funded through a commercial mortgage with a bank or financial institution, repayable over ten or fifteen years. It is a good longer-term capital investment; the premises are an asset on the balance sheet and, of course, there is no rent to pay. Full tax relief can be claimed on interest payments, and capital allowance can be claimed against the purchase cost. Very few small firms, however, have the spare cash or resources to find the 25 per cent deposit for the mortgage without selling or mortgaging their own private homes. Solicitors are essential for the conveyancing of freehold premises, both to ensure the legality of the process, and to check that no undeclared mortgages or charges exist against the premises, or planning consents which might adversely affect the site.

Leasehold purchase

Leasehold purchase provides a method of acquiring a capital asset for balance sheet purposes, without the same level of expenditure as freehold purchase. The business buys the leasehold rights to premises for a period of years (typically twenty-five, fifty or ninety-nine years on a new lease), and then pays the owner of the freehold rights an annual ground rent. The ground rent was traditionally paid on the four Quarter Days i.e. 23 March, June, September and December each year, although that tradition is now fading in favour of monthly direct debits. Once again, the deposit sums are usually around 25 per cent but, as the sum borrowed is lower than needed for freehold purchase, the repayments are more affordable. The repayment period is normally about fifteen years, as for most commercial mortgages, but could be longer for a long residual period or less if there are only a few years remaining on the lease. Leases can also be resold if the firm outgrows the premises.

The big drawback with selling leasehold property is that if a subsequent leaseholder goes bankrupt, the liability for outstanding and future ground rent payments can fall on the original or previous leaseholder. Again, solicitors are necessary for the conveyancing of leasehold purchases, and are essential for the checking of potential liabilities in the event of a future leaseholder defaulting on the lease, and the liabilities reverting to an earlier lessee. It is also worth checking for any restrictive covenants that may occur in leases for older buildings, as these could restrict the way in which the premises could be used.

Rental agreements

Medium or long-term rental agreements are quite popular on modern industrial estates and, sometimes, new businesses are enticed with an initial rent-free period of three to six months. Typically the agreement period will be for at least three years during which the monthly rent payment is fixed at a pre-agreed level. In longer-term rent agreements, the rent may be reviewed at specified intervals.

Short-term rental agreements are quite popular for very new businesses as they do not incur such long-term commitments as other arrangements. Typically rental agreements might be renewed year by year, with an annual rent review. The actual monthly or quarterly payments may be slightly higher than those of a medium-term agreement, but it is normally possible to terminate the agreements with between one and three months' notice. Another bonus is that the agreements do not require the involvement of solicitors and the associated fees. It is of course still advisable to get a legal or informed opinion (such as that of an estate agent or surveyor) before signing contracts for any rental agreement, in case of any adverse clauses hidden in the small print. It is worth paying particular attention to any clauses relating to the liability of occupants to pay for or contribute towards the upkeep and maintenance of premises. If these are included, then it is reasonable to expect the rents to be adjusted downwards to reflect the liability.

Other aspects of obtaining premises

The reader is reminded of the requirements for planning consent for change of use of premises under the Planning Acts, and the need for Building Regulations approval for any structural changes to premises or drainage etc. These are discussed in more detail in Chapter 5. Similarly, according to the nature of the use of premises, it may be necessary to obtain licences for specific activities from the local authority, under the Local Government Miscellaneous Provisions Act, and to register with the local authority for any food-related businesses under the Environmental Health Regulations.

Information about available premises can usually be obtained from commercial estate agents, most of whom are listed in *Yellow Pages*. Alternatively the local enterprise agency of bank business adviser may be able to suggest suitable options, and may well know of special incentives or assistance available to potential tenants.

There are basically three types of insurance related to premises – insurance for the building itself, insurance for fixtures and fittings, and insurance for stock of other contents:

What insurance cover will I need for the premises?

- Buildings insurance is taken out to cover the structure and fabric of the premises. It is usually the responsibility of the owner, i.e. the freeholder or leaseholder of the premises, and any person renting business premises should check to make sure that this is the case. The insurance covers the cost of repair or rebuilding work for any damage to the structure or fabric of the building by fire, storm, flood, acts of God and all-perils, e.g. from a runaway lorry crashing through the walls. It does not cover damage to anything inside the building, or to loss of trade during the rebuilding process. Cover for damage resulting from acts of war or terrorism is normally excluded.

- Building contents insurance excludes the structure of the building but covers all fixtures, fittings, furniture and equipment etc. within the building for a similar range of perils. For business premises it is normally prudent to keep an up-to-date inventory of all fixtures and fittings, office equipment, machinery etc., with original costs or values, to ensure that the buildings contents insurance is adequate to cover the cost of all contents. This form of insurance only usually covers permanent items of business property, excluding resale stock.

- Cover for the value of goods held in stock within premises is essential in case of fire, flood, theft etc. Most insurance companies are interested in the value of a realistic average level of stock, and policies will typically allow for seasonal increases in stock levels without extra charge. Again, check to make sure that the level of cover is adequate, as some insurance companies reduce the levels of payout if they believe the value of stock to have been underinsured.

What other types of insurance should I be considering?

- *Goods in transit insurance.* Following on from the previous item, any business involved in the sale and distribution of goods should consider goods in transit insurance. Premiums are normally based on the maximum value of each consignment (e.g. van- or lorry-load). Do not let the insurance agent try to set the premium against the total value of stock sold over the year, as this will result in a horrendous premium, and does not reflect the risk of the value of goods which could be lost in one incident.

- *Employer's liability insurance.* This is the only insurance which is required by law. Any business which employs staff must take out this insurance to cover its staff against accident or injury in the workplace.

- *Public liability insurance* is not compulsory, but is essential. It covers accident or injury to any member of the public or to their property.

- *Product liability insurance* provides you with cover against injury or illness affecting your customers or members of the public as a result of the use of your products. For example, food poisoning from food products or skin damage caused by beauty treatments.

- *Professional indemnity insurance* covers professional individuals against claims for negligence or misconduct, such as a hairdresser who uses the wrong concentration of bleach and causes the customer's hair to turn orange and fall out. Another example would be a design engineer who gets structural calculations wrong, and the structure he or she is building collapses.

- *Loss of profits insurance* is designed to provide an ongoing source of revenue when normal trading is interrupted due to some external factor. For example, if a fire damages a building and its contents stopping trade for two months, the loss of profits insurance would cover the expenses of paying ongoing overhead costs (rent, rates, insurance, staff etc.) until the business starts trading again. Payments are based on the calculated profits (not turnover) which have been lost. Good in principle, but it can take time to be paid out, and for new businesses without a trading record or previous year's accounts it can be hard to prove the real level of profits which have been lost. In the short-term, having this insurance should at least facilitate a temporary bank overdraft, to help until the insurance pays out.

- *Motor vehicle insurance* is essential for vans and lorries carrying goods, but also for private cars used in association with the business, for odd deliveries, visits to suppliers or customers or for carrying tools or work-related equipment.

- *Health insurance.* Private health insurance can provide a way to prompt treatment in private clinics, bypassing the National Health Service waiting lists. Good, but very expensive for better levels of treatment. The extent of cover is restricted in the lower bands. Health savings schemes are very cheap, and offer cash payments for periods of hospitalization, and other medical expenses.

- *Accident or long-term disability insurance* is designed to provide a pension-type income for people who become permanently disabled or unable to work as a result of serious illness or injury. Quite expensive for a good level of cover, but payouts only begin six months after the illness starts, and premiums have to be maintained in the meantime. Existing health problems are usually ineligible for consideration.

- *Key person insurance* is often required by banks when loans are made to partnerships. Apart from picking up lots of commission on the insurance premiums, this insurance is often linked to the loans so that the bank loans are automatically repaid if one partner dies. The other purpose of this is that it enables the surviving partner in a partnership, to buy out the share of the deceased partner, if the deceased's estate should require it. It can also be taken out on people who are key to the profitability of a business, and upon whose death the business would suffer financial loss.

- *Life assurance* is worth having to cover the value of any loans or liabilities of a business if the proprietor dies, to protect the inheritors of his or her estate. This can take the form of term assurance, i.e. flat rate payments for flat rate cover, with no payback at the end of the period. Term-with-profits insurance gives the life cover but for an additional premium pays back a lump sum at the end of the period of cover. Endowment policies are a longer-term savings-related form of life cover. Premiums are higher, but so are end-of-term payouts if you survive the term.

- *Private pension plans* are not insurance policies at all, but must be mentioned in the context of life insurance and personal financial planning. They are increasingly essential for anyone who is self-employed, and whose state benefits are therefore likely to be reduced. Self-employed people can claim tax relief against the pension contributions.

- *Combined policies* – often called shopkeeper's policies – are special insurance packages for various sectors of business. For example, a hairdresser's policy might cover a core package of employer's liability, public liability, professional indemnity, and theft and damage to equipment, linked together for a very competitive premium. There is also the option of extending the cover beyond the core parts for additional premiums.

Finally, insurance brokers deserve a mention as a means of obtaining fairly objective advice, and normally very competitive quotes, for business insurance. They earn their income (from the insurance companies, not from their clients) by matching the policies to their clients' needs and pockets. In recent years they have been hard hit by the growth of direct insurance over the telephone, but for small firms with widely varying insurance needs they can provide an efficient and cost-effective means of searching the insurance market for the right policy. Most of them are small businesses too!

Chapter 13 Physical
Chapter 13 resource
Chapter 13 requirements

Chapter 13 examines the ranges of physical resources which may be required in order to operate a business, e.g. plant and equipment, furniture, office machines and computers, stock, delivery vehicles etc., and the way these are purchased from suppliers and financed, the timing of their acquisition and the control systems used to monitor them. It also relates to contracts of supply with public utilities which may be different from those encountered in a domestic situation.

The objectives of Chapter 13 is to enable the reader to identify the range of physical resources which are likely to be relevant to his or her business in the early stages, to quantify these and to estimate their costs, to identify potential suppliers and the timing for acquisition. The resulting data will provide a valuable input into the budgetary forecast and cash flow forecasts for the first year of operation of the new business. This chapter also corresponds with the NVQ level 3 Business Planning Unit A9 'Assess the business needs for physical resources' which is concerned with identifying and quantifying the same resources, their costs, and implications for the finances of the business.

When people first start to think about the physical resources that they will require to start their businesses there is usually a tendency to underestimate both the range of items required, and the full cost of these. It is only when the likely full cost is realized that the same people start to ask themselves which items are really necessary as opposed to nice to have. The process also raises further questions about which items are needed from the outset of trading and which could be acquired out of profits as the business grows. In some cases it will be far cheaper to use existing resources which may also be available in the home, for example, do you really need a brand new computer for word processing, or will the old one at home do the job for the first few months?

Similarly, when looking at office furniture for example, new items may look impressive to customers but, if cash is short, it may be worth looking at second-hand alternatives which can still be of good quality and appearance, but which are often much cheaper. If the furniture is not in public view, it does not really matter anyway, so long as the furniture or equipment is functional and comfortable to use. The same principle applies to vehicles, as often it is cheaper to buy a two-year old van which still has a good potential life span, but for which someone else has already borne the cost of the substantial depreciation in value during the first year or so.

The important lesson to remember here is that without adequate working capital the business will struggle to get off the ground. If too much of your capital is tied up in resources which are not all in immediate or full use, then working capital may be tight, cash flow problems will arise and the business will be fighting to survive before it has had chance to become fully established. Equally however, we should not be sacrificing quality for the lowest price. As we have seen from Chapters 9 and 10, in the longer term a better quality but higher priced component may work out cheaper if it reduces the cost of rejects and customer complaints.

How do we identify what physical resources are needed?

First, we need to identify the broad categories of the resources, e.g. transport, fixtures and fittings, plant and machinery, furniture and office equipment, resale stock, raw materials and components, materials and consumables. The combination of the various groups will depend on the nature and complexity of the business. A manufacturing business will probably need most of these, except for resale stock, whereas a retailer or wholesaler will need to buy stock but will have no use for raw materials or components, and a mobile hairdresser will probably only need some basic transport and equipment.

The second stage is to brainstorm and list all the physical resources which could conceivably be required, and to sift through them eliminating those that might be nice to have at some point in the future, but which would not be essential for the first year of trading. Sorry, but the bright red Ferrari really must wait! The remainder can be sorted under three headings: 'Already available', 'Essential for start-up', and 'Buy during first year'.

The third stage is to go through the list and allocate realistic prices or costs to each item. These will be used to feed into the budgetary plan and cash flow forecasts described in Chapter 6. The planned acquisitions can be phased over the first year according either to how soon they are needed or to when sufficient profit is generated to pay for them. Minor items will probably be paid for at the time of purchase, but for major items of capital expenditure like machinery or vehicles, decisions must be made about how these will be financed. The need to obtain and repay loans to buy equipment, or the payment of hire purchase deposits and the subsequent phasing of payments for plant or vehicles, must also be accurately reflected in the budgetary plan and cash flow forecast. Some of the sources of funds and various options for financing the purchase of resources are discussed in Chapter 8.

Transport

The selection of vehicles required will depend not just on the type of goods or services that are being produced or provided, but on the distribution channels and the relative locations of the customers. If your goods are being sold to wholesalers who trade them on to a retail network, then large articulated delivery trucks might be the most appropriate form of transport. For the wholesalers themselves, medium-sized trucks, e.g. 7-tonnes, which can access narrower roads to reach the retailers are more appropriate. This size of vehicle is popular because it is not regarded as being a full heavy goods vehicle, and can be driven on an ordinary driving licence in the UK. If the customers are concentrated in a fairly close area, or if access is a problem, or if the goods are not too heavy, then vans with a payload of 1000–1800 kg are a better option, and unlike the 7-tonne options these do not even need to have a tachograph fitted. The choice of the type of vehicle and its payload or size is basically an operational one, but the decision to buy new or second-hand, or to lease or buy, will be determined by available working capital, interest rates on finance and the availability of the vehicles.

The same applies to cars, as the type of car (estate or saloon) will be determined by what it has to carry, the engine size by the fuel consumption and type of driving involved (local or long distance) and generally by what the owner-manager can afford. For example, a mobile hairdresser working locally might need an estate car or hatchback for ease of transporting equipment and, being local, a small economical engine would be fine. In this case it would not matter too much if the car were to be a few years old, so long as it was reliable. In contrast, if you were buying a car for a sales person to drive long distances around the country, you would almost certainly pick something new or nearly new for purposes of reliability. This may possibly be a saloon car so that samples could be kept out of sight locked securely in the boot, and with a 1.8 or 2.0

litre engine giving sufficient power for comfortable distance-driving.

Remember, when budgeting for vehicles, do not just think in terms of the costs of acquiring them, but allow for running costs such as road tax, insurance, MOT tests, repairs and maintenance etc., and build them into the budgetary plan accordingly.

Fixtures and fittings

These are essentially the items within the premises which are attached to the structure, or which are necessary to the production of the goods or services, but not directly used in their creation or provision. In terms of fittings we are talking about things like lighting and heating systems, electricity or water supply, telephones, sinks, toilets, etc., which have been fitted to the premises to make them habitable. It may be when moving into new premises that these are inadequate or need to be replaced or repaired. Perhaps extra power points are needed in the office, or the water supply has to be extended or new toilets built for additional staff. When considering these, you should think also of the installation costs as well as the purchase cost of the materials.

When we talk of fixtures, we are normally referring to items such as safety rails, storage or racking systems, lifting equipment, mezzanine floors, etc., which have been fitted or installed within the building, to facilitate the operation of the business. What fixtures do you need for immediate use, and what additions will be required as the business grows? Is it cheaper to install the whole lot from the outset or is this beyond the capital currently available? If you take out a loan for the additional requirements, will the savings on installation costs and later disruption to your business, outweigh the arrangement fee and interest payments on the loan? With storage facilities, we should

215

also be checking that not only are they of adequate size or capacity to meet current and forthcoming needs, but they are capable of being used in such a way to ensure proper stock rotation to avoid waste and additional expense. This includes ensuring that the environmental conditions, such as temperature and humidity, are suitable for the goods in storage.

Plant and machinery

There are many issues to be considered here, all of which will have a financial implication for budgets and cash flow. What essential plant or machinery is required to manufacture your products or processes? Do you have any of this, or can it be bought second-hand? If it is very specialized, will there be a long lead time for delivery? Will it take time to install and commission before becoming fully operational? Will the premises need to be modified to take it? Will you also need to maintain a supply of tools and spare parts for the machinery, and employ staff to maintain it? Will you need to make a substantial down payment when ordering it? How will you finance the period between ordering and becoming fully operational?

'Plant and machinery' not only includes things like production machinery, but items used in materials handling such as pallet trucks or fork-lift trucks, weighing, packaging and labelling equipment, pumps, cranes, lifts and pulleys, conveyor belts and rollers, power tools and hand-held equipment. There are also implications for insurance and the safe and secure storage of some of these items, particularly if they are valuable and easily moved (or removed).

Furniture and office equipment

This category will include not just the items within any management or administrative offices, but also the carpets, easy chairs, display material that may be located in a reception area for visiting customers and, of course, the tea and coffee cups, kettle, toaster or microwave oven for staff use.

Within an office we are including items such as desks, chairs, filing cabinets, storage cupboards, computers or word processors, a safe or petty cash tin, telephones, fax machines and answering machines, franking machines, cleaning equipment, and the multitude of minor items such as staplers, hole punches, rosaries and stress-relief toys. These are the things that are most often taken for granted or underestimated when planning a new business and, when compounded, their total costs can be quite high. They do, however, include items that the aspiring owner-manager may already possess.

Resale stock

Anyone involved in wholesaling or retailing will need to identify what stock has to be held at any one time. There will, of course, need to be a purchase of opening stock, and an ongoing holding of a reasonable level of core stock – those items that will be in constant demand. The costs of buying this opening and core stock have to be built into the budgetary plan. As stock is sold, more is bought in to replace it and to replenish stock levels and, as the business grows, so the average level of stock held may need to be increased. This can have implications for both storage space and equipment and for the availability of adequate working capital to fund the additional stock holding.

The frequency with which stock can be replenished, and the minimum order or delivery size from suppliers may also impact on the need for storage space and on the required levels of working capital. For example, a supplier based at some distance may only make periodic deliveries, so either a larger volume of the stock items have to be held or the retailer may have to pay additional carriage costs for intermediate deliveries. Some suppliers only offer free delivery where the order is above a certain minimum value, and others relate discount levels to the size of the order. Here the savings from free delivery and better discount rates have to be weighed against having extra working capital tied up in stock and the space which that stock is occupying.

Raw materials and components

This is a similar situation to the purchase and holding of stock for resale, only the initial purchase costs may be relatively larger, particularly if credit is given to distributors or customers. There is a need to buy an initial opening stock of raw materials and components and, whilst these are being turned into the finished product, further raw materials and components will need to be ordered to replace them. The wider the range of products offered, the greater the range of stock items will be, as will be the cost of buying them; once again as the business expands, so usually does the need to increase the average levels of stock holding. Depending on the source of raw materials and components, there could be implications for delivery lead times, especially if components have to be shipped from countries in the Far East that usually constitute one of the cheapest potential sources of supply.

Once again, the initial costs of buying the raw materials and components have to be realistically estimated, and the costs built into the budgetary plan and cash flow forecast for the business. The process would normally include identifying various alternative suppliers, the range and quality of their respective products, and their costs, discount structures and terms and conditions of trade. For example, given that product quality and basic cost of a component are the same from each of two suppliers, it may be that the extra 2 per cent discount offered by one is more than offset by the extra thirty days' credit offered by the other, if working capital is freed for use elsewhere. If, however, the discount were much larger, then it might pay the business to borrow money from the bank to pay for the components, as the costs of borrowing would be outweighed by the extra profit generated by the better profit margins. This is the sort of cost-benefit analysis that a bank manager will appreciate, and will normally be willing to accommodate. If adequate working capital is available, and interest rates are not excessive, then cash discounts beat credit terms any day.

Materials and consumables

These are the items that are purchased, used and replaced on a fairly regular basis as part of the administration or running of the business. In the office they would include stationery, envelopes, postage, computer disks, printer ribbons/cartridges, etc., and probably the tea, coffee, milk and sugar. In the working areas it might include the provision of protective clothing, safety wear or uniforms. In the business as a whole it would cover things like first-aid materials, cleaning materials, disinfectants, paper towels, toilet paper, light bulbs, the costs of a window cleaner, etc. In a large organization they would probably be accounted for under different headings, but in a small firm's accounts they might well be grouped together as 'miscellaneous and administrative expenses'. The accounting classification is less important than the fact that they should be identified and included in the budgetary plan and cash flow forecast because, although they are all quite minor items of expenditure, when aggregated and taken over a year, they can amount to a noticeable sum.

Public utilities

By these we mean the suppliers of electricity, gas, telephones, water supply, sewage disposal and waste disposal services. Most of us are familiar with these organizations through our domestic contact with them, but it is worth mentioning them in a commercial context as they are able to offer business customers more flexibility and competitive prices in some cases. Now that the supply of gas and electricity has been privatized and is no longer controlled by the former local monopolies (i.e. the former regional gas and electricity boards), business users can negotiate much more favourable terms of supply than were previously available. This is particularly relevant to those businesses with a large and regular or predictable demand.

Telephone services are now available from a range of providers, using conventional systems and cable networks. The systems providers can be highly competitive on price, and efficient in installation, although problems of interorganizational co-operation can often occur at the point where the various systems interface with each other, causing delays. These delays can be more critical for high-tech companies, or those relying on the Internet and e-mail marketing and communications.

In most parts of the UK the same water companies provide both water supply and sewage disposal services, for a single charge. In commercial premises this may be linked to size according to rateable value or, more frequently, to water meters installed on the premises. In some parts of the UK the water and sewage functions are provided by separate organizations, typically the small local water supply companies and the former regional water and drainage authorities. In these cases the charges are divided, although where water meters are installed, the supply company will usually pass on details of volumes used to the drainage authority.

What business users do need to be aware of is the fact that businesses that use high volumes of water as part of their production process or where waste water may be polluted, e.g. breweries and the paper industry, have a loading applied to their sewage disposal charges to cover the cost of reprocessing the waste water. For a new business these loadings may be imposed on an arbitrary basis, without actually testing the degree of pollution of the waste water. For example, when running a small brewery some years ago, I found that the metered water supply figures were passed on to the drainage authority. The latter allowed a 5 per cent reduction for evaporation, but levied a 20 per cent loading for contaminated waste. After challenging the loading and submitting several samples of waste water, the loading was reduced to 10 per cent, and the allowance was increased to 30 per cent on the basis that a fair proportion, having been consumed as beer, was recycled through someone else's sewer. It sounds daft but, in fact it, cut the annual sewage bill by almost 40 per cent.

Uniform business rates levied by local authorities have spiralled upward, and now constitute a significant overhead cost for most businesses. On the face of it, they do not actually buy you much apart from the access roads and site drainage, and even these may be subject to private maintenance for some business locations, although many local authorities do employ economic development staff to promote and support local enterprises. The council rates also no longer cover waste disposal unless you pay for it separately, and most firms now make private contractual arrangements with private operators who supply and empty bins on a regular basis. With the addition of taxes on landfill tipping, waste disposal is now becoming an expensive business, so allowance for this should be made in the budgetary plan, particularly if any of the waste products of your business are classed as dangerous or hazardous, e.g. poisons, oils or toxic chemicals. Above all you should be attempting to minimize waste to reduce these additional costs to your business. Recycling waste materials, and in particular packaging, will almost certainly become a statutory requirement at some time in the next few years, and it has already started in some industries.

It is important to remember that the public utilities are now mostly privatized, and you are one of their potential customers.

They no longer have a monopoly control over the market, and they themselves now have to answer to watchdogs such as Ofwat and Oftel. Do not be afraid to challenge them or to ask for better terms.

As a final note to this chapter, it is worth remembering several key points in dealing and negotiating with your suppliers:

Supplier relation-ships

- Your suppliers are just as much entitled to make a reasonable profit as you are. Do not be afraid to push them for a bit more when the time is right, but respect their position if they turn you down. They almost certainly still want your trade, but not at any price. Sometimes when a customer pushes too hard, you just have to walk away from the business if it is not worthwhile.

- The objective in dealing with suppliers should be to develop a long-term, honest and reliable relationship that will ensure continued supply of quality goods or services at a mutually acceptable price. The cheapest price is not always accompanied by quality and reliable products. It also pays to keep in regular contact with them, not only to find out about new products or opportunities, but to talk about any trends or changes in the marketplace which might affect you.

- If you have cash flow problems, do not lie to your suppliers or ignore their calls. They are not stupid and they can read the signs as well as you can. Be honest, contact them promptly and tell them about the problem, ask for their co-operation, and give them a firm and realistic date for payment, then honour it. If you can, make a payment on account in the interim period to show your goodwill. Sometime later it may be your supplier with a similar problem asking for a prompt or early payment, in which case, if you can afford it, help him out. This is what building long-term business relationships is all about, and it will do you no harm at all when a bank or another supplier asks you for a trade reference.

- Although price is important, it is not the only area for negotiation with suppliers. If the supplier is unwilling or unable to improve discounts or prices as the volume of your purchases increase, then look for alternatives, and be imaginative. Can you get better payment terms, e.g. a longer period of credit, or a higher credit limit? Is there some advantage to you in varying delivery arrangements, such as weekly instead of fortnightly to reduce the levels of stock that you need to hold? Will the supplier contribute to some of your marketing costs, e.g. by paying towards the cost of a trade exhibition, sharing advertising costs or by giving you some point of sale material or free samples for your customers? These are the sorts of possibilities that will benefit both you and the supplier.

- You should ensure that you have suitable monitoring systems in place to check on the quality of goods received, and that quantities, prices, discounts, etc. are correct. Any discrepancies should be recorded and notified to the suppliers immediately. You cannot realistically expect your suppliers to take responsibility for problems with goods that have been out of their hands for any length of time, so by reporting problems promptly you can avoid potential disputes. Again, be honest with them and do not try to rip them off by claiming more than is properly due. If your suppliers regard you as being fair to them, then they will tend to treat you fairly in future, and they will be more likely to respond to a request for help when you have a problem or need an urgent delivery.

Chapter 14 Recruiting
Chapter 14
Chapter 14
and employing
staff

Many people who are setting up a new business already have the technical and product knowledge that will enable them to produce or provide their goods or services. A smaller proportion of them will also have acquired some basic sales or marketing skills along the way. Some may also have been involved with staff management and supervision, including the recruitment and selection process. Normally, however, unless they have worked for a relatively small organization, they will have relied on the advice and support of a personnel specialist to guide them through the legal nightmare of the recruitment, selection and employment legalities and processes. Even before the advent of the European Union, this was not a matter for the faint-hearted, but nowadays the legal requirements and obligations demand an extensive and detailed knowledge of the subject to avoid the risk of overlooking the smallest of details.

I am sorry if this sounds like bad news but, quite simply, employing people is now becoming a hazardous and difficult procedure, in spite of repeated government boasts about how small firms will be the employment growth area of the future. The imposition of the European Social Chapter and various directives relating to working hours, minimum wages, leave entitlement etc., actually mean that employing staff is becoming an increasing nightmare in the UK, and yet in comparison with mainland Europe, the UK is still relatively employer-friendly. This is clearly evidenced by the sheer number of enquiries in recent years to Kent-based enterprise agencies from continental companies who still see the UK as a cheaper and more attractive option in employment terms, compared with employing staff in France or Germany where national insurance rates are over 40 per cent and where sacking even the most unsuitable of staff can be a costly and difficult process.

This chapter also relates to the NVQ Level 3 Business Planning qualification Unit A10 'Assess the needs for any additional personnel in the first years of trading'. This unit is concerned with planning the staffing needs of the business, assessing the impact of employing staff for the business operation, planning the process and programme of recruitment, and the subsequent appraisal and monitoring of staff performance. In reality it is very difficult to predict these needs beyond the first year, as there are simply so many variable and imponderable factors involved, particularly because of the very fact that it is the first year of trading. In later years, the planning and forecasting process should prove somewhat easier, once the new business has stabilized.

Politics and Europhobia aside, the objectives of Chapter 14 are to examine how to assess the personnel requirements of a business in its early stages, and how to go about the process of selecting and recruiting suitable staff. We have already examined the processes of skills gap analysis in Chapter 4, along with the personal skills and capabilities of the business proprietors. Where the skills of the owner-managers are either inadequate to meet the full range required, or where to utilize them would not be cost-effective (e.g. the owner-manager should not be typing letters or filing instead of selling the products or planning production), then it is appropriate to consider employing alternative staff. If we consider the primary objectives of the business, then the owner-managers' efforts should be focused on these and should not be spent on more mundane administrative matters which can be delegated to less expensive staff, who will probably do the job better anyway. Once we have carried out a skills gap analysis to determine questions of what skills or staff the business really needs, then, if those needs cannot be filled internally by delegation of staff development, it will be necessary to employ someone for that purpose.

The first of a number of questions that we must ask is whether of not we really need to employ staff. Do we have to employ them directly, or could we make use of casual, temporary or agency staff? Can we afford to pay the wages on a regular basis? Will the extra staff generate enough income to cover their costs, or will they release the owner-manager to spend more time working to produce extra profit? Will employing staff push up other overhead costs, such as insurance or protective clothing? Will there be a need for extra expenditure on furniture, machinery or equipment for them to use? Will there be enough work to keep them fully occupied? Can they be trusted in the owner-manager's absence? What will be the costs to the business or the effects on profit if they are not employed, e.g. will contracts be lost? How difficult or costly will it be to get rid of them if things go wrong? How soon will they be needed? What induction, training or supervision will be needed, and will this interrupt other work?

So, assuming that we have already identified the nature of the skills deficit and then asked and answered these important questions, we can start to look at the process of recruiting staff, and the further implications for the business.

The first implication of employing staff is the extra time and cost involved in meeting statutory requirements. In addition to the legal requirement to take out employer's liability insurance, once staff are employed there is the need to set up and maintain a PAYE (pay as you earn) system, to deduct income tax and national insurance contributions from the employees' pay, and to remit these to the Inland Revenue on a monthly basis. In addition to the deductions from pay, the employer must also pay an employers' national insurance contribution, currently 12.2 per cent of employees' pay, but which is subject to change in the Chancellor's annual budget. Staff are also entitled to be paid for holidays, sickness and maternity leave, and whilst away from work, other temporary staff still have to be paid to cover the absence. In addition to the financial implications, there are, as we have seen in Chapter 5, legal implications in terms of health and safety which have to be met, particularly once more than five staff are employed in the business. In the early stages of a new business there may only be a need for one or two employees, but as the business expands and extra staff are taken on, the legal implications can easily be overlooked, particularly if the owner-manager is not familiar with employment law or procedures. The significance of this may not be obvious immediately, but a year or two down the line, when the employees are protected from unfair dismissal etc., an overlooked issue may turn into an expensive industrial tribunal. It is important, therefore, that when staff are employed, their job descriptions and terms and conditions of employment should be clearly defined.

Of all of the resources utilized within a business, staff tend to be the least reliable in terms of the return they offer on the time and money invested in them. When a manager buys a piece of production machinery, the capital cost and expected annual running costs are known, as is the expected productive lifetime of the machinery. Unfortunately people are less predictable. The cost of recruiting staff can be high, and there is always an initial period of inefficiency when they are training or learning the job. Staff also have the annoying and inconvenient tendency to fall sick, to take holidays, to become pregnant or to leave for better pay elsewhere, and usually at the most inconvenient times. Is it any wonder then, that manufacturing industries prefer to use robotic systems on their production lines? Whoever heard of a robot suffering from PMT or taking an afternoon off to go to a football match? Seriously though, it is often hard to find staff who are willing to work hard and be committed to the business, and it sometimes even harder to keep them. Levels of commitment and motivation in staff are invariably linked to remuneration and reward – if you pay peanuts, you get monkeys, and the monkeys will soon move off to join someone else who is offering more peanuts. A business which has a continuous turnover of disaffected staff will never reach its full potential of efficiency or profitability, and will certainly suffer problems in achieving consistent standards of product quality and customer care.

To reiterate, recruiting and training staff is an expensive and time-consuming process and, in order for the investment in time and money to be recouped, it is essential to define most carefully the nature of the job and the type of person required. The recruitment and selection process should be a two-way situation. On the one hand it must be carried out objectively to match the candidates with the job requirements. On the other hand the remuneration package of the job itself, and the terms and conditions of employment, must be sufficiently attractive to the candidates to stimulate their initial interest in the job and to retain their services in the longer term. In this respect we are talking about job satisfaction and organizational culture, as well as pay and conditions, contributing to staff retention. For some people, high wages will adequately compensate for unpleasant conditions and boring work, whereas others will tolerate low pay for interesting work in a friendly environment.

The process itself typically falls into three stages:

- *Defining the requirements* – the job description, person specification, and the terms and conditions of employment.

- *Attracting candidates* – considering the use of internal promotion, training and development of existing staff, or advertising for external candidates and then choosing and implementing the most suitable means of finding candidates.

- *The selection process* – sifting the applications, short-listing, carrying out interviews, choosing the candidates, checking references, and making an offer of appointment.

In the case of new small businesses, this process tends to be somewhat simplified, first because there are rarely any internal candidates to consider for training or promotion and, second, because new owner-managers seldom have the suitable skills or time to spare for a full-blown recruitment and selection process. Unfortunately this can often result in the selection of candidates who may be less than ideal, especially if the job description or person specifications have not been produced carefully.

The job description

Once the decision has been made to employ a new member of staff, the first step must be to prepare a job description for the vacant position, which involves defining the scope, role and responsibilities of the job. The precise content of the job description will vary according to the complexity of the job and the levels of responsibility involved, but it might typically include:

- Job title and location.

- Grade or salary range.

- Position in the organization structure, and to whom the person is responsible.

- Main duties, i.e. the primary tasks, key activities, and the purpose of the job or the objectives the post-holder is expected to achieve.

- Main responsibilities, e.g. staff supervision, budget-holding, functional areas or processes.

- Supplementary duties, such as attending sales exhibitions, dealing with customer queries, health and safety, first aid (or in a very small firm, making the tea or even taking a turn at cleaning the toilets).

- Special job features, e.g. the need for regular foreign travel or to deal with foreign customers, anti-social hours or shift-work.

Whereas the job description is about the job itself, the person specification is about defining the characteristics, skills, qualifications, etc. of the type of person who would be ideally suited to fill the job. Bearing in mind the person specification would have to be non-discriminatory and compliant with equal opportunities regulations, this might include:

The person specification

- Age range, gender or marital status (if relevant or appropriate, but beware of anti-discrimination laws).

- Essential qualifications and experience.

- Essential skills, e.g. experience of managing staff or budgets, or specific technical knowledge or expertise.

- Desirable skills, e.g. the use of specific computer applications, possession of further qualifications, fluency in foreign languages.

- Physical health if, for example, the work involves heavy lifting or manual work.

- Essential behavioural competencies, such as the ability to work closely with a team of other people or to negotiate with customers.

- Desirable behavioural competencies such as a friendly disposition, sense of humour (especially if the pay is low!) or willingness to travel abroad at short notice, if needed.

Terms and conditions of employment

These must comply with legislation relating to contracts of employment, and would normally include:

- Job title.

- Duties, main and secondary, locations of work, flexibility and requirements to travel.

- Commencement date of continuous employment – important for the calculation of annual leave, statutory sick pay, maternity pay, and statutory redundancy pay entitlements, and to the dates after which the laws relating to unfair dismissal apply.

- Rates of pay (hourly, weekly, monthly, annual salary, etc.) and method of payment, e.g. cash paid weekly on each Friday, of by monthly bank transfer on twenty-eighth of month.

- Holiday or leave entitlements.

- Sickness arrangements, e.g. where the employer offers sick pay above and beyond the statutory requirements.

- Period of notice to terminate employment by either party, and the variations on this, e.g. suspension or summary dismissal for theft, violence or gross negligence.

- Arrangements for termination of employment, such as the return of vehicles or equipment, confidential information, or special arrangements such as 'garden leave' for sales staff moving to competitor organizations to avoid possible poaching of customers or theft of customer information during period of notice.

- Health and safety/discipline and grievance procedures – usually reference is made to standard organizational procedures, copies of which are supplied to the new employee on starting. In the case of new small firms, with less than five staff, these may not yet have been prepared.

- Workplace rules – these are not so much statutory regulations, as standards and procedures which are used within the workplace, e.g. standards of hygiene, no smoking rules, flexitime operation, logging of telephone messages and incoming mail, standards of dress when interfacing with the public etc.

- Trade union status or recognition – whether or not the organization recognizes a trade union or has negotiating arrangements with them.

- Special terms relating to inventions, patents, copyrights etc. for products or materials developed in the firm's time. These will normally belong to the employer firm and not the employee, unless special arrangements to the contrary have been made.

- Variations to contract – at the end of just about everyone's contract or employment there is a section which prescribes for variations to be made to the contract of employment, subject to a reasonable period of notice to the employee, etc.

Advertising the position

Internal promotion is always an option worth considering, and not just from the viewpoint of 'better the devil you know'. Existing staff are more familiar with the firm and its products and customers, internal recruitment is good for staff motivation (apart, perhaps, from the ones who did not get the job!) and the process is cheaper and less time-consuming. However, as mentioned above, in most new small businesses there will simply be no existing internal candidates to be considered for promotion or for training and development, so looking elsewhere is the only available option.

How do we go about finding suitable applicants? The first choice to be made is whether to pay someone else to do it or to do it ourselves. Advertising agencies have great expertise in designing and preparing advertisements and selecting the right places to advertise, but they also tend to have high fees and the potential success is still largely dependent on the detail and quality of the requirements specified by the client. Similarly, recruitment agencies have a great deal of expertise in finding and sifting potential applicants for short-listing, but they tend to charge between 20 per cent and 25 per cent of the first year's salary as their fee, which is not so good if the new recruit leaves within that year. Once again the usefulness of their results is also largely dependent on the depth and quality of the briefing by their client. In short, if you give them a poor job description and person specification, you cannot blame them if they do not come up with the right candidates for the job.

The other alternative is to do the advertising ourselves. For the newcomer to this type of advertising, unless he or she has skills in desktop publishing or computer graphics, it may pay to get some assistance. Some basic knowledge of designing advertisements, the use of logos, bold wording, margins and white space etc., can make a big difference to the impact of the advertisement on the readers. A recruitment advertisement should be treated the same as an advertisement for the firm's products or services, because it needs to catch the reader's attention and to prompt a response or action. Very often, the advertising staff at local newspapers can provide this advice as a service to clients. If given the basic job information along with a company logo and details etc., they will design the advertisement for an additional fee. Subsequent advertisements then becomes less costly as the basic artwork is already available. Assuming, then, that we have some basic idea of what we want to include in the advertisement, where should we place it, or where else can we find our suitable candidates?

For a fairly straightforward vacancy involving no specialist skills or expertise, a vacancy notice outside the firm's premises, a card in the local newsagent's window or at the local job centre all offer very low-cost options for finding staff at fairly short notice. As the level of necessary skills increases, then so does the importance of finding the right place to advertise. Local newspapers, particularly if they are part of a regional group, can reach a large readership in a concise geographical area, at a reasonable cost. Just how wide you advertise will depend on how far you think your staff will realistically be prepared to travel. For staff with high levels of skills or specialized qualifications and experience, it may well be necessary to consider advertising on a national basis, or in specialist trade magazines or journals, e.g. the *Times Educational Supplement*, the *Engineer*, the *Architects Journal* or the *Caterer* magazine. Of course, advertising on a national basis has implications for the cost of interviews, the possible need for new staff to relocate and the timescale in which the vacancy can be filled. Specialist staff are also likely to cost more and to attract special remuneration packages to retain them, which takes us back to the earlier option of whether or not it is worth promoting or training internal staff, and recruiting local replacements to fill their vacant posts.

In summary then:

- The method of advertising will be determined largely by the nature of the vacancy, and the local availability of likely candidates.

- The advertisement must be designed to attract attention, create interest and stimulate action and response from potential candidates. Applicants expect to be supplied with basic information about the job, the salary, the location and the employer organization. If the information is insufficient, then you may lose some good potential applicants. If you are unsure of how to design the advertisement, then it is worth getting experienced help or advice, even if you have to pay for it.

- The advertisement should tell the potential candidates precisely what action is needed and by when. For example, you should state clearly whether application forms will be provided for completion and return, or if applicants should send a curriculum vitae (CV) and letter of application. You should also state the closing date for applications and, if you do not intend to write to all applicants after that date, you should state in the advertisement the date by which applications will have been unsuccessful unless otherwise notified. This is both fair to the applicants and sensible from your perspective, otherwise, not only will your credibility as a potential employer fall in the eyes of some applicants, but there will be a proportion who will keep ringing up to find out about the progress of their applications.

- Once the advertisement is written, check for compliance with anti-discrimination legislation etc. and, again, if in doubt, seek advice.

- When the advertisement has been printed, measure the responses in terms of numbers of enquiries and applications, and the resulting cost per enquiry and per application. This will give you a yardstick against which you can measure the efficacy of future advertising, particularly if you have advertised in more than one publication.

Sifting and selecting the applicants

It is not uncommon these days to receive several hundred applications for one job, particularly if there is an attractive salary, and it is when we start to sift through all the applications that the usefulness of the job description and person specification really comes through. The process of sifting is quite straightforward, although it can be time-consuming if there are many applications to read and process:

- If there are a lot of applications, list them on a control sheet or database using a basic name and reference number, with space for a grading and comments.

● Discard immediate non-starters, e.g. those who have ignored basic instructions by sending a CV in place of your application form, or without the required covering letter, or with beer stains all over the application (yes, it does happen).

● Provisionally grade the applicants by one or two key criteria defined in the job description/person specification, e.g. essential qualifications and experience. Sort them into possibles, the long-list of marginals, the reserve list, and unsuitables which are rejected.

● Compare the possibles with further selection criteria to produce a short-list of likely candidates. If the list is sufficient then reject the reserves and if it is insufficient then re-examine the reserves. If the reserves are still inadequate then either something has gone wrong with the advertising process (the advertisement itself, or where it was placed) or you are simply not offering the right package to attract the calibre of applicants you require, or even both of these.

● Start the interview process using the short-list, which will hopefully produce a suitable applicant. If not, go back over your long list of marginals. If this is also inadequate, you have made a mess of it all, and its back to square one. So, where did you go wrong? Try to identify any mistakes that have been made, and review the alternatives.

Methods of selection

There are a host of various methods employed by larger organizations to select staff, including psychometric testing, personality questionnaires, three-day assessment centres, interview panels, aptitude or intelligence tests, handwriting analysis, 'informal' buffet lunches, selection boards, bio-data questionnaires, team skills activities etc. All these may be great fun to design or organize, but for the owner-manager every one of them is either time-consuming, or costly if carried out by someone else, and therefore detracts from the owner-manager's primary objective of keeping the business profitable to ensure survival and growth. So, for the majority of small firms, the obvious answer is to use the more conventional tried and tested options of one-to-one interviews supported by references. Even when very specific technical skills are involved, with a little preliminary guidance and advice, the owner-manager can normally find out ways of checking if the candidates have the necessary skills during the interview process. But one of the biggest advantages of face-to-face interviews is that they give both parties the opportunity to ask themselves the question 'Can I really work with this person?' and for the owner-manager, who is now in the role of the customer or buyer, to ask 'Will this person fit in with my business, and will they create the right image with my customers?'

However, although interviews are probably the most practical form of selection for a small business, for an owner-manager who has never carried out an interview before, the process can be as harrowing as for the person being interviewed. How, then, can we make the process easy to manage and less frightening?

Interviewing staff

The whole process of interviewing becomes less fraught if it is well planned and organized, and if we follow some simple basic guidelines. For example, before the interviews take place, the interviewer should:

- Give the candidates adequate notice of the time and date, with clear directions of where to go and details of overnight accommodation if needed.

- Tell candidates where to park and, if possible, make sure that there is space for them. On arrival, ensure that someone greets them, tells them where to wait and where

237

to find the toilets. Ideally, offer them a cup of tea or coffee, and sit them somewhere in private where they will not be subject to the scrutiny of any other staff.

- Look at the room layout, avoid barriers between you and the candidates, and try to create an informal and relaxed layout. If you put the candidates at ease, they are more likely to open up in discussion.

During the interview process:

- Ensure that there are no interruptions from telephone calls or visitors. If necessary put the telephone on answer service and leave a 'Do not disturb' notice on the door.

- Allow adequate time for each interview, and space between them to stretch your legs or to deal with any urgent calls. If you are using any tests or questionnaires, allow time for these to be completed, and time for them to be assessed before the candidates are interviewed.

- Plan the interview schedule to allow time for those travelling longer distances.

- Allow sufficient time for yourself, or any other interviewers, to read through the applications between each interview to remind you about each candidate and to highlight any specific questions you may wish to ask.

- When the candidate enters the room, introduce yourself and tell them briefly about your business and about the job. Keep it fairly short, then ask any standard questions you may have prepared and any specific questions relating to them individually.

- Invite the candidates to ask questions, encourage them to do the talking and listen to their answers. Use open or probing questions to encourage them to express ideas and opinions. If you are unsure of the answer, revisit it later in another way. Use hypothetical questions to assess the candidate's responses to possible problems, and closed questions to clarify a point or fact. Above all, do not talk too much.

- Make notes of candidates' answers and responses for later review.

- Finally, at the end of the interview, check that they are still interested in the job. Thank them for their time, and tell them when you will be making a decision and when you will notify them of the result.

After the interview:

- Review your notes, and consider some basic questions about the candidates. Think about the impression they have created on you, and whether or not you would want the same impression created on your customers. Will they fit in with you, other staff and the way your business operates? Can they do the job you want them to do?

- Compare the candidates against the job description and person specification. Which applicant met the requirements more closely? Would they fit in with your business? Do they still want the job?

- Check on references, make your decision, notify the successful candidate and make them an offer. If he or she accepts the offer, then notify the unsuccessful candidates. Always keep your notes of the interviews for several weeks, in case any of the applicants want feedback on why they were unsuccessful. If your chosen applicant falls through, you may even wish to go back to them.

Discipline and grievance procedures

Whereas most medium-sized and large organizations that can afford to employ specialist personnel staff, have written procedures for discipline and grievance, it is quite rare to find them in small firms, even though the risks and legal implications in

239

terms of industrial tribunals and appeals are the same. In fact the financial implications of a lost industrial tribunal, whilst they are an expensive nuisance to a big company, can be totally devastating to a small firm. Even winning a tribunal can still leave a business with hefty legal bills. It pays, therefore, to think about having some simple form of discipline and grievance procedures if you are thinking of employing even just a few staff.

The Code of Disciplinary Practice and Procedures in Employment describes the three basic principles of natural justice on which the disciplinary process is based:

1   Individuals should know the standards of performance that they are expected to achieve, and the rules to which they must conform.

2   They should be told promptly and clearly of how and why they are breaking any rules, or failing to achieve the required standards.

3   They should be given adequate opportunity to improve before disciplinary action is taken, or dismissal is implemented.

When disciplinary action is taken, if the offence is serious, e.g. it relates to theft, violence or dangerous behaviour that constitutes a major risk to health or safety, then an employee can be suspended and sent home immediately pending dismissal. Otherwise it is normal to take a three-stage approach involving an initial verbal warning (although with details recorded on file) after which, if there is no improvement, a formal verbal warning is given, usually with a letter which confirms the nature of the verbal warning. Finally, if the problem still persists, a formal written warning is given, with notification that further recurrence within a specified period of time will result in dismissal. The second and third stages are also recorded on file.

Grievance procedures tend to follow a similar pattern, depending on the size of the organization. In the case of a complaint, every employee is entitled to a fair hearing within a reasonable period of time. In a very small firm this may just involve a straightforward discussion with the boss to resolve the problem but, in larger firms, it may involve successive appeals to higher levels of management through a standard procedure, e.g. supervisor, line manager, senior manager or director. It may also involve colleagues, personnel staff or trade union stewards over a period of several days. In either case there has to be a cut-off point at which the process stops. It is always worth keeping on file a record of the process at each stage, for later reference.

A large proportion of tribunals is based on dismissal or, more to the point, unfair dismissal. Dismissal by means of the formal period of notice or upon expiry of contract is quite fair but if, for example, the employee is refused work after pregnancy or is unjustifiably demoted, this may constitute constructive dismissal, which is illegal. Two key questions are asked by tribunals in these circumstances:

1   Was there sufficient reason for dismissal, i.e. was it fair or unfair?

2   Did the employer act reasonably or unreasonably in the circumstances?

Staff appraisal

There are still some managers who regard it as regrettable that the P45 has been superseded as the primary form of staff appraisal, and there are still some staff around for whom it remains the most appropriate method. In the past two decades, staff appraisal systems have become almost universal within large and medium-sized organizations. Formal systems are still relatively rare in very small businesses, apart from those which have implemented more formal quality systems such as IIP or

ISO 9000, or where the owner-managers have come from larger businesses where appraisal was an accepted part of the organizational culture.

Appraisal is essentially a process of performance management. The basic principle is that every member of staff has a private and uninterrupted interview with their immediate superior or manager on a regular basis, e.g. annually or half-yearly. Prior to the interview, both parties will typically complete a form in which the manager reviews the performance of the staff member over the preceding period, and the staff member reviews their own performance over that same period. The two assessments are then compared and discussed. The appraisal process is meant to provide a constructive analysis of performance, which can be used to set targets or objectives for the forthcoming period, and which are agreed by both parties. It is also used to identify any areas for staff development or training, either to redress weaknesses or to prepare the person for a future extension of their job role. It is an opportunity for praise as much as for criticism, and should certainly not be regarded as a mechanism for punishing staff. In many organizations, it is also used to form the basis for pay reviews or promotion.

In order for it to work properly the appraisers are normally provided with training in listening skills, and how to handle the interviews in an objective and non-threatening manner to put the appraisee at ease and facilitate a useful and productive dialogue. An autocratic style of management is not exactly conducive to achieving quality discussion in appraisals, where open and honest discussion is essential. A good appraisal system will encourage feedback from both parties on the relationship and interactions between each other. It should also be welcomed by employees, not feared or dreaded.

Further reading

Armstrong, M. (1995). *A Handbook of Personnel Management Practice*. Kogan Page.

Clayton, P. (1998). *Law for the Small Business*. Kogan Page.

Palmer, S. (1998). *People and Self Management*. Butterworth-Heinemann.

Stokes, D. (1998). *Small Business Management: A Case Study Approach*. Letts.

Thompson, R. and Mabey, C. (1994). *Developing Human Resources*. Butterworth-Heinemann.

Warwick, J. and Francis, C. (1999). *You and Your Business Series: People*. SFEDI.

Chapter 15 Formulating the business plan

Chapter 15
Chapter 15

In Chapter 2 we examined in some detailed, an example of business plan layout which would satisfy the requirements of most bank managers or financial institutions, and which would also facilitate the evidence requirements of the NVQ Level 3 in Business Planning.

The purpose of this chapter is to briefly revisit the subject for the benefit of NVQ candidates in the context of the specific requirements of Unit A11 of the NVQ qualification. However, this process would not be wasted on any potential owner-manager who is going through the motions of formulating his or her business plan, as Unit A11 is designed to encourage the business planner to pause and take a step back to re-examine the work they have carried out so far.

Element A11.1 is headed 'Review the research you have carried out'. Now why on earth would I want to do that when I have only just finished it? Well, quite simply, the process which we have been working through in the preceding chapters has been very much a piecemeal exercise, researching and analysing specific individual aspects of the business. We have looked at the financial planning and controls, the marketing, resource requirements, premises, skills analysis, staffing, insurance, relevant legislation, etc. We are now, for the first time, in a position to assemble the components of the plan and to look at complete picture of the business as a whole. So let us make sure we have got it right.

In this respect, the performance criteria within Element A11.1 of the NVQ provide an excellent and comprehensive check-list, requiring the business planner to:

- Review all the data gathered during the research process about the business, its requirements and its markets, to ensure that the resulting information is both accurate and correct. This is an eminently sensible and obvious suggestion.

- Review all the financial research and figures, checking them for accuracy, and ensuring that they are still relevant and not in need of revision. It is so easy to make minor changes within the business plan as it is developed, and then to fail to adjust the final calculations to reflect those changes. Perhaps, for example, you have decided to employ an extra member of staff within the business, or to revise the sales revenue without adjusting your cash flow forecast. Murphy's Fourth Universal Law of Cock-Ups states that you can be certain that the very item you have failed to adjust, will always be the first one that the observant bank manager chooses to ask you about.

- Ensure that the reviewed data enables the reader of the business plan to clearly identify the objectives of the plan, and that those objectives are realistic within the context of the plan. This is partly a matter or the style of presentation, in ensuring that the objectives stand out within the business plan. But it is also a matter of producing reasoned argument backed up by factual data, to justify to any potential financial backer, that the objectives are both realistic and achievable.

- Review the sources of the information that you have used, to ensure that the information is still up to date. This is particularly important where, for example, calculations have been based on current interest rates or exchange rates. It would also apply to any overheads and materials costs which have been included in your budgets. Are they still current, or have they increased for any reason?

- Confirm with any potential lenders, funders or backers that their requirements will remain the same, i.e. that they have not changed the terms or conditions of their funding or support or their expectations of returns from the business. It can sometimes take a long time from first devising an idea for a new business to the stage when the final details of the business plan are produced, and many things can happen during the intervening period. It is also important, therefore, to double-check that that none of your backers or financiers has had second thoughts, or have invested or tied up their money elsewhere in the meantime. If there is likely to be any substantial delay, it is often worth asking them for a letter of intent, which confirms their interest and support for your proposals, subject to negotiation of final terms and conditions, and the signing of formal agreements etc.

- Finally, when you have checked and reviewed your data and information, update or correct your business plan to reflect any changes that have occurred. If those changes have been substantial, you should identify any significant impact they might have on your proposed operations, and refer to this in the business plan. Will they affect the marketing of your goods or services, or your turnover or profitability? Will they impede or interfere with the way in which you plan to operate and, if so, how will you deal with this problem? Will you need to change or improve your control systems to manage the changes? Will you need to employ any additional staff or resources, and what are the cost implications? If you have already completed your business plan, you may wish to show this information as an addendum or an appendix to the plan, along with any published data or information which might support your modifications to the business plan. Do not be put off by thinking that by adding extra bits on to the end, it will detract from the overall appearance or impression of your business plan. If anything, it will add to your credibility by showing that you are perceptive to changing influences and that you can respond to them and revise your plans accordingly. In the world of small business, flexibility and adaptability are the keys to survival.

Element A11.2 of the NVQ qualification is concerned with the actual production of the business plan. The content and layout of the plan has already been detailed in Chapter 2, but Element A11.2 is not so much concerned with ensuring that all the relevant business plan headings have been included, as in emphasizing the need for the business plan to be logical and coherent. Again, this is as relevant to any other business planner as it is to the NVQ candidate. The performance criteria require the candidate to ensure the following steps have been taken:

- The various component parts of the business plan should be integrated to form a coherent document which is consistent throughout, and which contains no self-contradictions or discrepancies in facts or figures. It should be comprehensive but concise, factual, honest and accurate. It is often a good idea to provide an abstract or overview of the document (300–400 words is sufficient) which summarizes the business idea, its potential profitability and the key points of its implementation. If your financiers have requested a particular format for the plan, then so be it. It may well be the case that they employ some form of scoring system which assists in evaluating the relative merit of the plans which they receive, or that the specific format helps them to utilize the criteria which they apply to approve applications for funding.

- The business plan should clearly state the nature of the business, its feasibility within the marketplace, the necessary resources required for start-up, its revenue, cash flow and profit forecasts. It will also need to identify the key personnel and their respective roles, and to show the way in which it will be managed and organized. This information is not just for the benefit of potential backers, but as an ongoing management tool for the owner-manager of the business.

- The plan should also show how and when the plan will be implemented, including the identification of any key or critical stages of implementation. It must also analyse any potential risks, and propose the contingency plans that would be used to handle them if they occurred during the implementation of the plan.

- Finally, the plan should contain sufficient information to allow any potential financier or backer to make a reasoned decision about its viability. Remember, key information should be included within the business plan itself, whilst supplementary or secondary information is best referred to and included in an appendix to the plan.

It is intended that this book should meet the needs of both the potential owner-managers who are planning to start a new business, and those who are pursuing the NVQ Level 3 Business Planning qualification, or possibly both at the same time. It must be said, however, that the 1999 revision to the NVQ Business Planning Standards have resulted in a sensible and comprehensive structure which is eminently usable, whether you are bothered about achieving the qualification or not, and Unit A11 is particularly good in this respect.

When assembling your business plan ready for submission to the bank manager or financier, it pays to give careful attention to the quality of presentation. You should aim to create an impression of professionalism in the way you present your proposals. The document itself should be prepared carefully, and should comply to certain basic minimum standards:

- The document should be bound in some form of flexible binding. Most high street stationers can offer a wide range of inexpensive transparent or coloured plastic bindings used for reports, dissertations and business plans.

- At the front of the business plan you should provide a header page which states clearly the name of the business and the proprietor(s). For example, 'Business Plan for Acme Wedding Services. Miss Helen Highwater. November 1999'. The main title of the business should be centred, about one-third down the page, in large bold letters (20–24 point). The name of the proprietor(s) should be lower down, to the left-hand side, and in smaller letters, e.g. 14 point, with the date of preparation opposite on the lower right-hand side of the page.

- Immediately inside you should provide a brief contents page, listing the key sections of the plan. It is also useful, if the business plan is a lengthy document, to provide a short summary or abstract which describes briefly the nature of the proposal, as suggested above.

- The bulk of the document should be word-processed or typed (handwritten documents do not create a professional image) on single side A4-size paper, with margins of at least 1 inch/2 centimetres all round. It is usually best to use either white, or a light coloured, paper for ease of reading and always use a good quality paper of at least 80 or 90 grams per square metre (gsm). Single spaced lines are quite acceptable, although it is a good idea not to make paragraphs too long. If you have word-processed the document, do not forget to use the spell-check, otherwise, proofread it carefully as, again, silly typing or spelling mistakes do not create a good impression. Spreadsheets and tables should also be checked for silly errors. The use of bold text is quite acceptable to emphasize key points, especially if they contain favourable or impressive profit forecasts.

249

- Any bulky supporting information or research material not directly relevant to the main content of the business plan should be confined to the appendices. Whilst it is useful to have such data available for reference, too much indirect information within the central text can be distracting and may well deter the reader from moving on to the important parts of the text. The use of coloured diagrams is has become standard practice in recent years, but they should be included to show relevant data only, and not simply to impress the bank manager with your computing skills (unless, of courses, that is the nature of your business).

- Finally, it always pays to have one or two spare copies available, in case the bank manager has mislaid the one you sent or perhaps in case of accident. It does not create a good impression to proffer the bank manager your one and only copy covered in beer stains, and a second copy is always useful for reference when you are asked questions. If you really do only have one spare copy, then either wrap it securely in waterproof material or avoid tea, coffee, wine and any other coloured food or drink which will invariably be drawn to it like a magnet, and just stick to clear gin or vodka!

Chapter 16　The NVQ assessment process

Chapter 16
Chapter 16

The history and purpose of NVQs

National Vocational Qualifications and the equivalent Scottish Vocational Qualifications (SVQs) have been with us since the late-1980s. The 1986 government White Paper 'Working Together: Education and Training' led to the formation of the National Council for Vocational Qualifications (NCVQ), recently replaced by the Qualifications and Curriculum Authority (QCA), to create and operate the NVQ system.

National Vocational Qualifications were originally intended to offer a framework of assessment by means of which working people who had no formal or academic qualifications could achieve formal recognition of their competence or expertise in a particular vocational area. More specifically in the field of Business and Management, it would enable self-taught managers, who may perhaps have been successfully running a business or a functional area within an organization, to provide evidence of their competence in that field and receive acknowledgement of their skills and abilities. Furthermore, the NVQ process would, by virtue of its structure, provide benchmarks for the assessment of competent work, along with the opportunities to develop and implement standards of best practice.

National Vocational Qualifications have frequently been criticized and often unfairly maligned by those who do not fully understand the ways in which they operate (particularly by members of more academic institutions). We still occasionally hear the remark: 'NVQ stands for Not Very Qualified!' and NVQs have also been branded as second-rate qualifications. In the initial stages of their development, that opinion may have been partly justified, as there was certainly opposition to the concept of NVQs, along with an initial lack of interest and support for them, from academic bodies. They quickly gained popularity, particularly amongst a range of smaller and often private providers who found them easier to deliver than established qualifications, although in some cases the standards of delivery and assessment was perhaps less rigorous than conventional educational institutions. The survival and existence of many of the smaller training providers was often governed by the need to achieve a profit, which was made much harder by the TEC-controlled funding systems which were geared to results defined in terms of job-filling rather than completion and achievement of the qualifications. In short, whilst the principles behind the extension and expansion of the NVQ system received heavy government support, the practicalities of government employment policy often worked against them and, obviously, this contributed little to enhance the standing and reputation of NVQs in the eyes of the public and employers. Fortunately, those days have largely gone, and the NVQ is now being increasingly accepted and recognized as an acceptable alternative to conventional qualifications, particularly in the workplace.

One of the factors that contributed to the misconception of NVQs as second-class qualifications was the fact that, unlike conventional examinations and methods of assessment, NVQs could be assessed in a variety of ways, e.g. by portfolio, observation, audio or video tapes, witness testimony etc., the variety and disparity of which made the establishment of consistent standards of assessment much harder to achieve. Over a period of time the lead bodies that establish the NVQ standards, and the accrediting bodies that operate them, have been able to produce a comprehensive and consistent framework of benchmarks and guidance by means of which assessors and verifiers can achieve and maintain consistent quality of delivery and assessment of NVQ programmes. In turn, the employers whose staff have undertaken NVQ programmes have increasingly come to regard them as an acceptable educational 'currency' of comparable value to conventional qualifications. The NVQ process is aimed not just at the achievement of a qualification, but at helping candidates to improve their performance in the workplace by embracing examples of best practice.

Much of the obscure and difficult wording of the NVQ standards, which was often a feature of the earlier qualifications, has been replaced with more readable and understandable language; and the way in which the standards are interpreted for assessment purposes has become much more consistent and user-friendly. Probably the biggest indication of their acceptance is that whereas in the earlier days of NVQs financial subsidies from the government had to be used as an incentive to raise the levels of uptake of NVQ training, the NVQ qualifications now tend to sell themselves to potential users. At one time TECs were offering subsidies of up to 50 per cent to firms that signed-up their staff for NVQs. Nowadays, such support is hard to find unless linked to achievement of IIP, and even then, the available subsidies are less than before. In short, NVQs have carved out their niche in the educational market, and look like being here to stay, without the need of financial incentives to encourage their uptake.

So, how do NVQs work?

In order to answer this question, we first have to explain the structure of NVQ qualifications.

First, NVQs operate at different *levels* (see Figure 16.1), starting at Level 1 where the qualifications are quite basic, and progressing through to Level 5, where complexity and detail renders them comparable to degree or postgraduate level qualifications. Although it must be emphasized that it is simply not possible to make a direct comparison between NVQs and

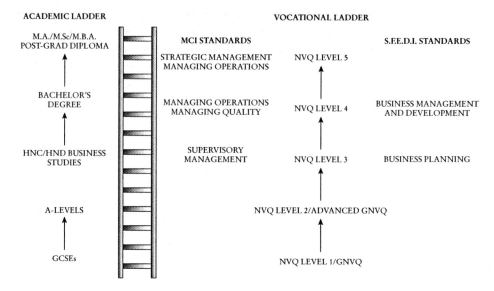

Figure 16.1 Comparison of academic and vocational training progression

conventional qualifications, most people find the concept much easier to comprehend if the two systems are viewed alongside one another.

Imagine two ladders, each with five rungs, standing alongside each other against a wall; but with the rungs of each ladder spaced at different intervals to each other so that no one rung is at exactly the same height as its counterpart on the other ladder (Figure 16.1). The academic ladder starts with GCSEs, and progresses up through A level GCEs, HNC or HND, Bachelor's Degrees, and Postgraduate Diplomas or Masters' Degrees. These are assessed by conventional means, such as essays, assignments, examinations, projects, dissertations etc. The vocational ladder has Levels 1 to 5, and a person's progression through these levels is assessed by their achievement of the specified standards of competence at each level; with those standards becoming increasingly more complex and difficult as the ladder is climbed. The important difference between the two ladders is that the person on the academic ladder, who is operating in a learning environment, has to prove learning of knowledge at each level in order to proceed to the next rung. However, the person climbing the vocational ladder, who is usually operating in a working environment, has to prove both knowledge of the job and competence in doing the job, in order to complete that level.

Let us take management qualifications. For example, an acting or potential supervisor might typically study for a Certificate in Supervisory Management, which could lead on to a Certificate in Management, and progress to a Diploma in Management or, ultimately, to a Master of Business Administration. The supervisor would not necessarily have to gain promotion to a higher level of management in order to achieve success in the higher qualifications if he or she were academically capable. However, in order to achieve the NVQ Level 3 in Supervisory Management a person would actually need to be working in a supervisory capacity of some sort in order to provide the necessary evidence to prove that they could meet the competencies specified in the vocational standards. Similarly, that person would need to be acting at line manager level in order to achieve the NVQ Level 4 qualification, and at a more senior management level to complete Level 5. Within the NVQ structure, the experience of actually doing is recognized as being a substantially relevant part of the process of achieving the qualifications, and the assessment process is designed to measure the extent of that experience.

The vocational standards for each level of NVQ are divided into *key roles*, which indicate the main functional groupings of the vocational standards. For example, the NVQ Level 3 Supervisory Management specifies four key roles: Managing Activities, Managing Resources, Managing People and Managing Information.

The key roles in turn are divided into *units*, which focus on more specific aspects of the key roles. Again, in the case of the key roles of the NVQ Level 3 Supervisory Management, the key role of Managing People is composed of the 'C' units:

Unit C1   Manage yourself.

Unit C4   Create effective working relationships.

Unit C7   Contribute towards the selection of personnel for activities.

Unit C9   Develop teams and individuals.

Unit C12   Lead the work of teams and individuals to achieve their objectives.

Unit C15   Respond to poor performance in teams.

The NVQ units at each level are subdivided, this time into *elements*, which focus on more specific aspects of the units. Hence Unit C1 of the NVQ Level 3 Supervisory Management becomes:

Element C1.1   Develop your own skills to improve your performance.

Element C1.2   Manage your time to meet your objectives.

The elements in turn are subdivided into *performance criteria*, which comprise the individual statements for which the NVQ candidates must provide evidence in order to demonstrate and claim their competence. In the case of Element C1.1 there are six individual performance criteria, prefixed by the instruction: *You must ensure that:*

C1.1a)   You assess your skills and identify your development needs at appropriate intervals.

C1.1b)   Your assessment takes account of the skills you need to work effectively with other team members.

C1.1c)   Your plans for developing your skills contain specific, measurable and realistic objectives.

C1.1d)   You undertake development activities that are consistent with your plans for developing your skills.

C1.1e)   You obtain feedback from relevant people and use it to enhance your performance in the future.

C1.1f)   You update your plans for developing your skills at appropriate intervals.

Alongside the performance criteria, the vocational standards specify *range statements* which describe ranges of circumstances or situations in which the candidate is expected to demonstrate competence, e.g. how many times the candidate must evidence a performance criterion, or what special circumstances must be taken into account. A good example of this is found in the Internal Verifier Unit D34, in which the D34 candidates must demonstrate how they have supported assessors who are dealing with assessment of students with special assessment requirements. Here the range statements require the Internal Verifier candidate to provide evidence of three different cases, which might perhaps involve students with learning difficulties, disability, dyslexia, etc., or simply lack of opportunity for assessment.

Finally, the vocational standards specify *knowledge requirements* against which the NVQ candidate must demonstrate the knowledge and understanding that underpin the activity being assessed. Some assessors use a range of preset questions that the candidate must answer. I prefer to encourage the candidate to write a personal report for each unit, which acts as a descriptive link between the evidence and the performance criteria. Within the report the candidates explain their role and involvement with the evidence, and how and why the evidence satisfies the criteria. This approach elicits the underpinning knowledge from the candidate, and the assessor can then ask the candidate specific questions about any apparent gaps in the underpinning knowledge. The personal report approach assists the candidates to identify and 'claim' their own competencies.

Overall, this approach is conducive both to the achievement of consistently high standards of assessment, and to facilitating the candidates to demonstrate their competencies.

Do the owner-manager NVQs work the same way?

The short answer is 'Broadly, yes they do'. In terms of NVQ levels, the NVQ Level 3 Business Planning operates at the same level as the NVQ 3 Supervisory Management, and it is one of the unique features of the NVQ system that the modular unit structure allows individual units from one NVQ qualification to be mixed with, or taken alongside, those of another. For example, the original NVQ Level 3 Business Planning Units incorporated Unit A7 'Evaluate own performance', which was directly lifted and incorporated from the Training and Development NVQ Level 3 Unit C21. In turn, the recently devised vocational standards for reflexology and aromatherapy have adopted five of the NVQ 3 Business Planning standards in order to cover the competencies required for self-employment status of most working complementary therapists whose profession is covered by those standards. Similarly, two of the NVQ3 Supervisory Management units are found within the NVQ3 Training and Development structure. An added bonus is that the possession of NVQ units achieved under one qualification in which they are used, allows direct exemption, termed 'accredited prior learning' (APL), from equivalent units in other NVQ qualifications. In theory, then, a person who holds the NVQ 3 Supervisory Management with the required units, and who is an accredited NVQ assessor and internal verifier, could claim APL for five of the nine Training and Development NVQ Level 3 units. In practice though, that person would still have to demonstrate to their assessor that those competencies for which APL is being claimed, are still currently practised.

Candidates who have previously been involved in operating or managing a small business may also be able to claim 'accredited prior achievement' (APA) where it is directly relevant to the new business. For example, if the candidate has specific

258

The revised owner-manager standards

experience of one or more key areas (such as sales, accounts or debt collection) which are appropriate to the new business, then a letter from the previous employer testifying to the candidate's skills and experience can form a valuable piece of portfolio evidence.

The revision of the Level 3 Owner-Manager (Business Planning) vocational standards took place during 1999. The new standards, effective from spring 2000, and to which the preceding chapters are linked, are much more detailed than the previous standards, and allow the NVQ candidates more flexibility in tailoring the qualification to match the nature of their own proposed businesses. There are now have eleven units in place of the original seven, although candidates still only have to complete six units to achieve the full qualification.

The revised standards also have much less emphasis on range, and each unit is divided into six sections:

- The national standard.

- The performance criteria.

- Knowledge requirements for the unit.

- Assessment for NVQ and SVQ, and for best practice.

- Details of evidence requirements for assessment of the unit.

- Examples of evidence appropriate to meet the evidence requirements.

Although these headings are slightly different from the standard structure of NVQs, they do cover the same material, as the detail prescribed in the evidence requirements effectively spells out the range that must be satisfied. Overall, the revised standards are much more user-friendly and easier to follow, as they provide the candidates with specific and useful guidance of how to produce evidence which will satisfy the performance criteria.

Taking Unit A3 as an example, Element A3.1 'Define the needs for setting up the business as a legal entity' requires the candidates to show that they have examined the various trading status options (sole trader, partnership, limited company, etc.) and made a reasoned and justifiable choice as to which is most suitable. The performance criteria require the candidates to research the options, to consider their impact on potential customers and suppliers, to examine the impact of any future change in trading status, to define the reasons for their chosen option and to ensure that the chosen status conforms to legal requirements. By explaining the reasons for their choice within the business plan the candidates not only satisfy the performance criteria, but they also demonstrate their knowledge and understanding of the options. By further referring to the tax, planning, health and safety implications etc., of their choice within the business plan, the candidates can demonstrate that they have researched the statutory requirements that are relevant to their business, thereby satisfying the evidence requirements for Element A3.1.

How does NVQ assessment work?

As stated earlier, whereas conventional qualifications use essays, assignments, tests, examinations, projects, dissertations, etc. to assess whether or not students pass or fail their courses, the NVQ process is fundamentally different. National Vocational Qualification candidates do not 'pass' or 'fail'. They are either competent or not yet competent. Note that because a person has not yet proved their competence, this does not imply that they are incompetent. The competence may be achieved in the near future or in the more distant future, depending on when the candidate has the opportunity to provide appropriate evidence. For example, the fact that a supervisor does not get involved in recruiting staff does not mean that he or she is incompetent or not competent at that task. Given the opportunity to become involved in the recruitment process they will have the opportunity to test and prove their competence, but until such time as such an opportunity arises, it is not appropriate to judge or comment on their competencies in that area.

When a candidate is assessed for their NVQ qualification, they produce evidence to demonstrate or prove that they meet the requirements of each of the individual performance criteria statements within each NVQ element and unit. This evidence may take the form of reports, written statements, photographs, letters, memos, audio or video tapes, witness statements or direct observations of performance. Typically, direct observation is more appropriate to NVQs at Levels 1 and 2, where more practical skills are involved. At Levels 3, 4 and 5 the processes are often more cognitive than practical, so a different form of assessment is more suitable. For example, you can observe the process of someone competently shaping a loaf of bread or changing a car tyre; but you cannot observe the processes and competencies involved when a manager makes a decision, as most of it goes on in the manager's head.

The evidence presented by the candidate is examined by a trained assessor who is both a qualified expert in the field in which the candidate is being assessed, and holds the NVQ assessor's qualification (Training and Development NVQ Units D32 and D33).

The most common form of assessment, particularly for business and management NVQs, is by means of a portfolio in which the candidate assembles their evidence, and explains, by means of a personal report, how or why the evidence proves the candidate's competence for each of the performance criteria.

Advice in the preparation of the portfolio evidence is often given by the same assessor, or by a separate adviser – frequently the NVQ tutor or a person who holds the Training and

Development Unit D36, which relates to advising candidates to identify their achievements and on the APL.

The completed portfolio, when assessed as meeting the required standards, is then examined by an internal verifier from the same institution or training centre as the assessor. The internal verifier is responsible for checking the assessor's work and standards of practice to ensure fairness, consistency and to maintain high standards of assessment, as well as supporting and advising the assessor, and acting as the link between assessors and the awarding body. The internal verifier will hold, or be working towards achieving, the Training and Development Unit D34.

Having been checked by the internal verifier, a group of completed portfolios will then be sampled by an external verifier who holds Training and Development Unit D35. The external verifier is appointed by the awarding body, e.g. City and Guilds, IoM, OCR, London Chamber of Commerce and Industry (LCCI), NEBSM, Institute of Personnel and Development. The awarding body will provide the candidate with the NVQ certificate to show that the qualification has been successfully completed and achieved, when the achievement has been confirmed by the external verifier. The external verifier liaises between the awarding body and the individual NVQ centres, which deliver the NVQ programmes, and is responsible for ensuring the maintenance of high standards of assessment within those centres. The external verifier must also ensure consistency of assessment standards across the groups of NVQ centres for which the awarding body is responsible.

To reiterate then, the vocational standards are designed by national training organizations (formerly lead bodies or amalgamations of them), and are accredited by Awarding Bodies such as City and Guilds, IoM, OCR, etc. The candidates for NVQs are assisted to prepare the evidence of their competence by advisers, and the evidence is assessed by qualified assessors, and subsequently checked by internal verifiers and external verifiers, who also hold qualifications in the appropriate areas of expertise. Indeed, with the proper assessment and verification procedures in place, the process as a whole is as thorough, rigorous and consistent as any conventional academic qualification.

What constitutes a good NVQ?

Some training providers still take the NVQ principle at face value, as just an assessment process, whilst others combine the assessments with a full programme of tuition and support. When looking for a suitable training provider for the NVQ Level 3 Business Planning, you should ask a range of questions:

1   Does the NVQ qualification offered by the training provider include a planned programme of workshops for underpinning knowledge and portfolio building, or does it just provide essential documentation and assessment? The workshops or lectures should provide comprehensive coverage of the NVQ knowledge requirements and preferably additional practical information, e.g. basic understanding of taxation, VAT, credit control etc.

2   Does the programme offer tutorial support? It is important to have someone to talk to, or telephone, if you have problems in formulating your business plan, collating items of evidence or preparing personal reports. A knowledgeable tutor can save valuable time – both yours and the assessor's. The tutor, who may also be the NVQ assessor, should act as the primary adviser to the candidate, giving support and guidance in the preparation of suitable evidence for assessment.

3   Does the training provider have a successful track record in providing the NVQ Level 3 Business Planning and other NVQs? An established centre will normally have documentation and systems in place to assist you with the completion of the NVQ. The tutors and assessors

will also be familiar with the vocational standards and evidence requirements. Good advice on the presentation of suitable evidence can again save a great deal of time writing, assessing, changing, reassessing, correcting for yet more assessing etc. Most people who take the NVQ Level 3 Business Planning are intending, or at least considering, starting up their own business and, therefore, it is the completion of the business plan as opposed to the NVQ assessments that is of paramount importance to them. Similarly, as much as bank managers like to see that a potential customer has a business planning qualification, there is nothing like a sound business plan and a detailed budgetary plan and cash flow forecast to stir them.

4   Have the tutors had any direct experience as owner-managers of small businesses? This may seem like a silly question, but it never ceases to amaze me how many business tutors have no actual business experience and how many trainers contracted by TECs, or employed by Enterprise Agencies, are retired middle managers from large companies, local authorities or public utilities who just assume that what is appropriate for large organizations, will suit small firms. The training requirements of owner-managers are very different from their counterparts in big companies, as they need a much wider range of skills to succeed in business. The average owner of a small firm is also the accountant, sales person, production manager, credit controller and, often, the van driver and toilet cleaner as well. Big companies can afford long-term strategic planning, but for most small firms survival is the primary objective in the early days, and forward planning is measured in months rather than years until the company is well established and financially stable. Pressure of work and shortage of time leads to reactive rather than proactive management. Most small business people have to learn by their mistakes and, having done so, their experiences are most valuable to people who are

just about to embark on their first enterprising venture. Accountants may understand the mechanics of running an efficient small business, but only an owner-manager can describe the pressures and practicalities involved, from their own personal experience.

5   Is the assessment process clearly defined? Are you aware of what will be required and how you will need to present your evidence? Tales abound of less experienced assessors who pile on demands for more and more evidence to ensure that everything is adequately covered, largely because they are too inexperienced to differentiate between good evidence and insufficient evidence. The NVQ assessment process is not intended as a paper chase – one or two good pieces of evidence will suffice for any performance criterion, and most items of evidence can be used against quite a number of them. Ideally, the evidence presented for an element should relate to as many of the performance criteria as possible, so as to construct an overall picture of the candidate's competence, rather than a piecemeal itemized description. This is often described by assessors as the story-book approach, where the candidates use the evidence to paint a picture in the assessor's mind of their competence. It is also important that the assessment documentation is easy to read and follow, as this can vary widely from one awarding body to another. Onerous checklists of range statements etc. can distract the candidate's attention from the main objective, which is to produce a viable and usable business plan not just for the NVQ, but for the business itself. Some training providers produce standardized business plans where the candidate just fills in the boxes. These may be of assistance in achieving the NVQ, but not only do they stifle any individual flair and imagination, they are not conducive to producing a finished document which can be lifted out of the portfolio and presented directly to a bank manager or potential lender. Unfortunately, possession of

the NVQ Level 3 Business Planning does not convey with it automatic survival in the marketplace. However, possession of a good business plan can at least point you in the right direction.

In summary, a good training provider will provide you with clearly defined and easy to use assessment documentation. It will offer practical and useful training that will be of relevance to the new owner-manager, preferably delivered by someone with direct knowledge of the small business environment. It will provide guidance and support in the preparation and assessment of the portfolio but, most important of all, it will facilitate preparation of a viable business plan in a format and style that can be presented to a bank manager without modification.

Institute of Management – Certificate in Management (Business Start-up)

This programme of study has been designed for those people who prefer the conventional means of assessment rather than the NVQ process. It can be taken as a stand-alone qualification or in conjunction with the NVQ in Business Planning as a double qualification. Although available on a distance-learning basis, participants are encouraged to meet together with other aspiring entrepreneurs to exchange ideas and information, and to discuss their problems.

The syllabus of the Business Start-up Certificate covers basically the same underpinning knowledge requirements as the NVQ programme, although its contents are covered in slightly more detail, and delivered in a different format:

1.1 Entrepreneurship (generate the business proposal).

1.2 Financing the business (progress the business proposal: establish financial requirements).

1.3 Business planning (prepare the business plan).

1.4 Marketing the business.

1.5 Management of the business (managing, monitoring and controlling business operations and quality).

1.6 Legal requirements (progress the business proposal: establish legal requirements).

1.7 Personnel planning (personnel planning and development).

The Certificate in Management (Business Start-up) is awarded to candidates who have completed assessments for the above seven modules, along with an overarching project, e.g. the production of a comprehensive business plan that covers most aspects of the syllabus. It is intended as a personal and professional development programme for those people who are either about to start a new business, or who are in the early stages of new business development. It is perhaps best suited to those who might become self-employed in the more distant future, but for whom the production of a business plan is more of an academic exercise in the near future. For example, the vocational students who need to understand the process of business planning, but whose immediate need is the completion of their vocational studies.

Further reading

Walton, J. (1996). *The NVQ Handbook: A Practical Guide for Providers and Assessors.* IoM and Butterworth-Heinemann.

Appendix 1 Summary of Units and Elements of the revised Owner Manager NVQ Standards

A1* Assess the potential of the proposed business

A1.1 Describe the proposed business.

A1.2 Review the market.

A1.3 Evaluate the likelihood of success with the proposed business.

A2* Assess your own skills and capabilities for running the business

A2.1 Identify the skills needed.

A2.2 Analyse and evaluate your own skills.

A2.3 Devise your own self-development plan.

A2.4 Monitor your own performance.

Note: * denotes a mandatory unit. Each candidate must complete four mandatory and three optional units to achieve the full NVQ/SVQ award. Additional units can be taken if desired.

Small Firms Enterprise Development ment Initiative Owner-Manager Standards for NVQ/ SVQ Level 3 Business Planning

A3 Investigate the requirements of any legislation you have to comply with in setting up and running the business

A3.1 Define the needs for setting up the business as a legal entity.

A3.2 Define the operational controls to ensure the business operates legally.

A3.3 Assess the impact of health and safety and associated legislation on the business operation.

A3.4 Assess and use sources of information and advice.

A4* Establish how you will finance the start-up and keep track of money once the business is operating

A4.1 Assess the financial requirements to set up the business.

A4.2 Identify how the business will be funded.

A4.3 Provide financial forecasts and explain what financial controls you will use.

A4.4 Identify how you will measure financial performance.

A5 Develop a strategy for marketing and sales

A5.1 Analyse the market for the products and services of the proposed business.

A5.2 Develop the marketing plan for the business.

A5.3 Develop the sales plan for the business.

A5.4 Specify how the success of the marketing and sales plans will be assessed.

A6 Investigate ways to ensure that the business operates to quality standards

A6.1 Assess the importance of a quality focus in the business.

A6.2 Identify ways to incorporate quality into all aspects of business performance.

A6.3 Define quality targets for the business.

A7 Establish a customer service policy

A7.1 Assess customer needs.

A7.2 Develop a policy for procedures to meet customer needs.

A7.3 Specify how the policy will be put into practice and its effectiveness monitored.

A8 Assess the business needs for dedicated premises

A8.1 Evaluate the business needs for premises.

A8.2 Select premises which meet the business need.

A8.3 Establish your business terms for negotiating and agreeing contracts for business premises.

A9 Assess the business need for physical resources

A9.1 Identify the physical resources needed by the business.

A9.2 Evaluate supply options.

A9.3 Develop a schedule for obtaining and maintaining physical resources.

A10 Assess the need for any additional personnel in the first years of trading

A10.1 Identify the personnel needs of the business.

A10.2 Assess the impact on the business of employing staff.

A10.3 Develop a plan for recruitment, training, work allocation and performance appraisal.

A11* Develop a comprehensive business plan

A11.1 Review the research you have carried out.

A11.2 Produce the business plan.

C12 Lead the work of teams and individuals

MCI Standards for NVQ/SVQ Level 3 Supervisory Management

C12.1 Plan the work of teams and individuals.

C12.2 Assess the work of teams and individuals.

C12.3 Provide feedback to teams and individuals on their work.

D1 Manage information for action

D1.1 Gather required information.

D1.2 Inform and advise others.

D1.3 Hold meetings.

The two MCI units are considered of potential use to new owner-managers who may be new to staff supervision, communicating with clients and staff, and running business meetings. If appropriate, these units can be taken in addition to the owner-manager units.

Index

Index

Index